Entrepreneurial Leadership

Entrepreneurial Leadership

Strategies for Creating and Sustaining Partnerships for K-12 Schools

Shelley B. Wepner and Diane W. Gómez

ROWMAN & LITTLEFIELD
Lanham • Boulder • New York • London

Published by Rowman & Littlefield
An imprint of The Rowman & Littlefield Publishing Group, Inc.
4501 Forbes Boulevard, Suite 200, Lanham, Maryland 20706
www.rowman.com

6 Tinworth Street, London SE11 5AL, United Kingdom

Copyright © 2020 by Shelley B. Wepner and Diane W. Gómez

All rights reserved. No part of this book may be reproduced in any form or by any electronic or mechanical means, including information storage and retrieval systems, without written permission from the publisher, except by a reviewer who may quote passages in a review.

British Library Cataloguing in Publication Information Available

Library of Congress Cataloging-in-Publication Data

Names: Wepner, Shelley B., 1951- author. | Gómez, Diane W., author.
Title: Entrepreneurial leadership : strategies for creating and sustaining partnerships for K-12 schools / Shelley B. Wepner and Diane W. Gómez.
Description: Lanham, Maryland : Rowman & Littlefield, 2020. | Includes bibliographical references. | Summary: "This is written for K-12 educational leaders to help them develop and use their entrepreneurial skills to cultivate partnerships with businesses, community organizations etc"—Provided by publisher.
Identifiers: LCCN 2019041725 (print) | LCCN 2019041726 (ebook) | ISBN 9781475846515 (cloth) | ISBN 9781475846522 (paperback) | ISBN 9781475846539 (epub)
Subjects: LCSH: Educational leadership—United States. | School administrators—Professional relationships—United States. | Business and education—United States. | Public-private sector cooperation | School and community—United States.
Classification: LCC LB2805 .W435 2020 (print) | LCC LB2805 (ebook) | DDC 371.2—dc23
LC record available at https://lccn.loc.gov/2019041725
LC ebook record available at https://lccn.loc.gov/2019041726

Entrepreneurial Leadership Is about Good Relationships

To my late father Bernard Markovitz, a small-business owner, who taught me about the multifaceted nature of entrepreneurial leadership.

To my husband Roy; and daughters, sons-in-law, and grandchildren—Meredith, Judd, Eliza, and Sydney Grossman; Leslie, Marc, Teddy, and Sloane Regenbaum—who continue to enlighten me about the boundless joy of loving relationships.

From Shelley

To my husband David, an educational leader in higher education, who epitomizes the meaning of partnership personally and professionally.

To my daughters, sons-in-law, and grandchildren—Cristina, Ivan, David, and Idalia Calderon; Julia; and Victoria, Steve, and Steven Wood—who lovingly demonstrate life is all about relationships.

From Dee

Contents

Foreword	xiii
Acknowledgments	xvii
Introduction	xxi

PART I: ENTREPRENEURISM AND PARTNERSHIPS   1

1 Entrepreneurial Recognition of Partnership Opportunities   3
   Characteristics and Evolution of Entrepreneurial Leaders   4
   Entrepreneurial Leadership in K-12 Schools   5
   Rationale for Entrepreneurial Leadership in K-12 Schools   5
   Examples of Entrepreneurial Leadership Partnership Pursuits
      in K-12 Schools   6
   The Importance of Entrepreneurial Leadership for Forming
      Partnerships   8
   Definition and Benefits of Partnerships   10
      Benefits for Students and Parents   11
      Benefits for Teachers and Administrators   15
   Partnerships, Entrepreneurial Requirements, and the
      Educational Experience   19

2 Partnership Types   21
   Motivation for Partners to Get Involved in Schools   22
   Three Types of Partnerships   23
      Businesses   23
      Communities   24
      Colleges/Universities   25

Why Businesses Form Partnerships with Schools	26
Workforce Competitiveness	26
Good Will	27
Good Publicity in the Surrounding Community	27
Why Community Organizations Form Partnerships with Schools	28
Community Health	29
Community Well-Being	29
Culture of Good Citizenship	30
Why Colleges and Universities Form Partnerships with Schools	31
Preparation of New Teachers	31
Sites for Teaching College Courses	32
Research	32
Recruitment of Students and Faculty	33
Potential Partners' Outlook on Partnerships with Schools	34

3 Guidelines for Entrepreneurial Leaders in Building Partnerships — 37

First Steps in Moving a District Forward	37
Thinking and Acting Entrepreneurially	39
Gathering Data to Create Elevator Speeches for Potential Partnerships	40
Examples of Elevator Speeches	40
Major Areas for Data Collection for Possible Partnerships	42
Students	42
Teachers	43
Parents	44
Community	45
Curriculum	45
Resources	46
Begin Your Plan for Developing Partnerships	48
Work with a Group of Like-Minded Individuals	48
Find and Communicate with Potential Partners	49
Establish Partnerships	50
Identify Key Person(s) Responsible	51
Seek Approval	51
Execute Written Agreements	52
Adjust Arrangements to Accommodate Multiple Partnerships	59
Create a Blueprint for Implementation and Evaluation	59
Provide and Ensure Preparation and Training for Partnership	59

Communicate with the Community	60
Develop System for Assessing Outcomes	60
Recognize Partners and Participants Publicly and Privately	63
Reflections on Entrepreneurial and Strategic Planning for Partnership Engagement	64

PART II: REAL-LIFE BENEFITS OF PARTNERSHIPS 67

4 Partnerships with Businesses 69

Reasons School-Business Partnerships Work	70
Use Local Business Organizations to Create Pathways to Partnerships	71
U.S. Chamber of Commerce	71
National Federation of Independent Businesses	72
Connect with Local Businesses and Alumni	72
Reach Out to Alumni	73
Core Values for Working with Businesses	74
Administrator's View on Partnerships and Core Values	74
Commercialism in the Schools	75
Partnerships for Fund Raising	76
Stop and Shop's A+ School Rewards Program	77
Pursuing Fundraising Opportunities	77
Partnerships with Product Donations	81
Partnerships to Promote Attendance	81
Partnerships to Promote Students' Eyesight	81
Partnerships for Teachers' Professional Development	82
Partnerships with Employee Volunteerism	82
Service to the Schools	83
Mentoring	84
Partnerships to Support Secondary Students' Career Readiness	85
High School Career Academy's Approach to Partnerships	85
Guidelines for Forming Partnerships with Businesses	86
Creating Opportunities with Businesses	89

5 Partnerships with Communities 91

Create Pathways for Community Partnerships	92
Community Schools	93
A Bit of History	95

National Youth Service and Development Organizations	96
Girl Scouts	96
Boy Scouts of America	97
4-H Clubs	97
National Alliance for Youth Sports (NAYS)	98
Boys and Girls Clubs of America	98
Community-Based Organizations (CBOs)	100
Educational Organizations and Programs	100
Health Organizations	101
Social Service Organizations	102
Government and Military Agencies	103
Faith Organizations	104
Sororities and Fraternities	104
Cultural and Recreational Organizations	105
Individual Community Members	105
Creating Community Partnerships	106
Consider a Full-Service Community School	107
Leadership to Organize and Create a Community School	108
Leadership to Form Community Partnerships	109
6 Partnerships with Colleges and Universities	**111**
Possible Partnerships with Colleges and Universities	112
Types of Partnerships	113
Type 1: School-College/University Partnerships	114
Type 2: School-College/University School of Education Partnerships	116
Type 3: Professional Development Schools-College/University Partnerships	117
Promises and Challenges	119
Promises	120
Challenges	121
Create Pathways for Forming Partnerships with Colleges and Universities	125
7 Sustaining Partnerships	**129**
Understanding Sustainability	130
Reasons for *Not* Sustaining Partnerships	132
Relationship with Partners	132
Deliverables in Relation to Goals	134
Impact on Stakeholders	134
Guidelines for Sustaining Partnerships	136
Entrepreneurial Leadership Orientation	136
Mutual Understanding and Expectations	137

Constant Communication 138
Continuous Monitoring of Conflicting Expectations 139
Facilitation of Two-Way Flow of Activities 140
Measures of Success 140
Considerations for Revisiting and Renewing Partnerships 142
   Use Outcomes to Determine Short- and Long-Term
     Opportunities 142
   Co-Construct Next Steps with Partners 144
   Students as Beneficiaries 144
The Importance of Entrepreneurial Leadership for
   Successful Partnerships 146

References 149

About the Authors 163

Foreword

Shelley and Diane's book, *Entrepreneurial Leadership: Strategies for Creating and Sustaining Partnerships for K-12 Schools*, has arrived at a perfect moment, and I am delighted that they asked me to write its foreword.

The noted community organizer, activist, and educator, Joy Dryfoos, has always been an inspiration to me. Some refer to Joy as the "mother of the community school" because of her work to build meaningful collaborations between schools, social service agencies, and health professionals—particularly in communities plagued by poverty and all the issues that poverty brings with it. Joy understood, long before most, the power that partnerships can provide to our schools and to our schoolchildren.

"Full-service community schools," Joy once said, "have the capacity to bring together in one space the resources and personnel that can strengthen both the school and the community." She was, of course, right. Today's community schools address the needs of the "whole child" in a comprehensive way, enabling students to access the kinds of services they need to perform their best in school and in life: academic, health, mental health, dental, vision, hearing, nutrition, adult literacy, legal, and after-school services, among many others. Because these critical services are offered in one convenient place, under the school's roof, it is much more likely that students and their families will utilize them. Simply put, community schools help to level the playing field by blunting the insidious effects of long-entrenched racial and economic inequality.

But community schools represent a major shift in how we think about running our schools. They require systemic change in operational philosophy. That kind of change can be difficult. They require us to relinquish control and to depend on one another. They require us to develop strong community partnerships that give community-based organizations, students, parents, families, and businesses a voice in decision-making and planning. But they work—and that is why the transformative power of the community school model has informed so much of my work as a school administrator and a policy-maker.

In 1995, I took over as principal of Washington Heights Intermediate School 218 in the northernmost section of Manhattan. Like much of New York City, Washington Heights has experienced tremendous gentrification in the last twenty or so years. But in the 1980s and 1990s, the neighborhood was rife with poverty, crime, gangs, and drugs—especially crack cocaine. It was a community in crisis. I knew before I ever stepped into that school that we had to change the culture at IS 218 if we were going to give the children there a fighting chance to succeed.

So, working together with the Children's Aid Society, we immediately set out to establish the kind of community school experience envisioned by Joy. Focused on educating the whole child, we offered parents a place to send their children before and after school—a place where they could participate in activities ranging from remedial reading to teen pregnancy prevention, from theater to volleyball.

But that wasn't nearly the extent of it. With funding generously provided by Alianza Dominicana, the After School Corporation, the National Institute for Community Schools, the Alvin Ailey Dance Company, Learning Leaders and others, we were able to create an institution within the school that combined academics with health services, youth development activities, and parental involvement. Because good health is inextricably linked to a child's ability to learn, we built an on-site clinic with free medical, dental, and counseling services. And because so many students lived in households where their parents, grandparents, or other guardians weren't always around, we kept the school open fifteen hours a day, six days a week, and twelve months a year. The school became a refuge, a safe haven for countless children in need.

I learned many important lessons at IS 218. Perhaps most important, I learned that, as principal, I didn't have to do everything by myself; I didn't have to try to solve every problem on my own. Shared responsibilities bring better results for students and families. We all have a stake in our communities, so we all have a role to play in improving them for the benefit of our children. It's not an overstatement to say that our future depends on it. To this day, I remain very proud of the role I played in helping to create and bring to fruition New York City's first-of-its-kind full-service school.

Today, I have the incredible honor to serve as Chancellor of the New York State Board of Regents, New York's education policy-making board. And I continue to draw inspiration from Joy's belief that all students can succeed if we build, sustain, and grow meaningful collaborations. Regardless of whether they are wealthy or poor; large or small; urban, suburban, or rural—schools need strong partnerships with local businesses, community organizations, and higher education to address their students' needs in a comprehensive way.

Through their book, Shelley and Diane help us to understand that we are all in this together and that, by bringing together the resources of an entire community, we truly can reach every child in our care. They deserve nothing less from us.

Betty A. Rosa
Chancellor of the New York State Board
of Regents and Regent for the Twelfth
Judicial District (Bronx County)

Acknowledgments

We are in a profession that is all about helping young people, yet we often are held back by budgetary constraints to do what is needed. Educational leaders with entrepreneurial proclivities have discovered that there are people outside their schools who are willing to contribute their time, services, and funds to help students succeed. We acknowledge these educational leaders because they were the impetus for this book.

These K-12 entrepreneurial leaders shared their uplifting stories about their search for and cultivation of business, community, and college/university partners. Their stories are woven throughout the book to demonstrate how they have added riches to their schools.

We especially thank the K-12 principals, directors, and superintendents whom we interviewed or observed:

- Justin Aglio, Director of Academic Achievement and District Innovation at Montour School District in McKees Rocks, Pennsylvania
- Marc Baiocco, Superintendent of Elmsford Union Free School District, New York
- Cassandra Lewis Davis, Principal in DeKalb County School District, Georgia
- Mary Foster, Assistant Superintendent of Peekskill School District in Peekskill, New York
- Scott Mastroianni, Principal of E. P. Foster STEM Academy of Ventura, California
- Sue Ostrofsky, Principal of Fox Lane Middle School in Bedford Central School District, New York
- Ray Sanchez, Superintendent of Ossining Union Free School District, New York

- Rosa Taylor, Principal of Park Avenue School in Port Chester School District, New York
- Traci Walker, Principal of the Eliot K-8 Innovations School in Boston, Massachusetts.

We thank Felix Flores, a former principal and now the Professional Development School Liaison for Woodside Elementary School in Peekskill School District, New York, for helping us to understand how he used a college/university partnership to promote parent engagement.

We thank three leaders of nonprofits who helped us to appreciate their motivation for working with schools:

- Emily Keating, Director of Education for the Jacob Burns Film Center in Pleasantville, New York
- Marcia Oglesby, Grants and Partnership Coordinator for DeKalb County School District, Georgia
- Jeannette Shulz, the Lead for K-12 Stem Initiative for Amgen Foundation in Thousand Oaks, California.

We also thank Christoph Winkler, Endowed Professor and Founding Program Director of the Hynes Institute for Entrepreneurship & Innovation at Iona College in New Rochelle, New York, for enlightening us about the notion of entrepreneurism and educational leadership.

Our main gratitude goes to Tom Koerner, Vice President and Publisher of The Education Division for Rowman & Littlefield Publishing Group. Once again, he is the *one* person who believed that we had something worthwhile to say. He gave us the hope that we needed to forge ahead in writing about the value of entrepreneurial leadership and partnerships in K-12 education. We are deeply appreciative that Tom recognized that this topic had a place in Rowman & Littlefield's library of professional books.

We genuinely appreciate the added support from managing editor Carlie Wall and associate editor of production Christopher Fischer at Rowman & Littlefield. We also thank project manager Monica Sukumar at Deanta for her assistance.

We thank graduate assistant Dana Leon for her conscientious and skillful approach to identifying research, reaching out to our interviewees, and assisting us with the many big and small tasks related to writing this book. Finally, and most importantly, we thank our spouses for their steadfast love and support.

Shelley's spouse, Roy, continued to live with a wife who creates makeshift offices—replete with a laptop, papers, and food—wherever and whenever they travel so that she could take advantage of her "free" time to work on this book. His unconditional love and brilliant guidance continue to enable Shelley to persist during the most frustrating moments.

Dee's husband, David, pitched in to do whatever was necessary to keep the home front harmonious while Dee strove to meet deadlines. His constant, loving encouragement kept her going throughout the writing and editing process.

I (Dee) thank Shelley, my dean and colleague, for the writing partnership we share. I am humbled and thankful for her leadership and mentoring through our writing journey. She knows when to push me and when to lay back. Her eagle-eyed editing and attention to detail are amazing. I feel honored to call her my mentor and friend.

Introduction

Entrepreneurial Leadership is written for K-12 educational leaders who understand their critically important role as motivators, influencers, and entrepreneurs. These are leaders who have a mindset for pursuing opportunities that positively impact their organizations. They understand that, while they do not have to focus on the amount of money that they bring in each day, they do have to focus on measurable achievement outcomes for their students. They know that they need to go beyond their own institutions to see and seize opportunities that will bring resources and services to their schools to help their students achieve.

This book describes how such K-12 leaders can use their entrepreneurial skills to form partnerships by working creatively and diplomatically with external networks and resources. It helps school leaders learn how to tap into their strategic, social, and organizational skills to develop relationships and pursue partnerships that provide additional help, funds, and resources for their community of stakeholders.

Entrepreneurial Leadership is a "how-to" book for forming partnerships with businesses, communities, and colleges and universities. It uses real-life examples from different types of schools and school districts to demonstrate how partnerships can help to solve problems, offer new opportunities, and uplift a community.

General and specific guidelines are provided for school leaders inclined to innovate so they can initiate, develop, implement, evaluate, and sustain partnerships. Such partnerships can be with individuals, groups, institutions, organizations, and corporations at the local, regional, statewide, and national levels. Policies, procedures, and practices for effective negotiations within school systems and with potential partners, all critical for those with entrepreneurial tendencies, are included throughout the book to promote enriched opportunities and noteworthy successes.

REASONS FOR WRITING *ENTREPRENEURIAL LEADERSHIP*

The K-12 community can benefit from forming partnerships with local, regional, statewide, and national groups, businesses, institutions, and organizations that want to and can provide human and material resources. Some of these entities already have as their mission to help schools, while others realize as a result of outreach from the schools that they have resources that will assist schools.

Leaders of K-12 schools should use their entrepreneurial skills to capitalize on various partnership opportunities. These opportunities include instructional assistance for students, physical and medical health care for students, professional development for teachers, administrative assistance for leaders, guidance for parents, career internships and mentoring for students, and materials and equipment for the school.

In order to take advantage of partnership prospects, entrepreneurial leaders need to use their "can do" orientation to

- identify needs within their schools and districts;
- develop innovative ideas and solutions;
- become aware of possible partnerships in their own neighborhoods and beyond to help with these ideas and solutions;
- develop policies, procedures, and practices for establishing partnerships;
- negotiate effectively with potential partners; and
- create systems for evaluating and sustaining partnerships so that they truly are helping their K-12 community.

Partnerships can be as simple as the formation of an after-school tutoring club for second graders created by a faculty member from a local college or as complex as a university takeover of a school. Partnerships can involve local businesses or national corporations. When partnerships provide mutually beneficial opportunities, whether short-term or long-term, they enrich the lives of those involved and the culture of the organization in unanticipated ways.

Entrepreneurial school leaders can bring to their schools and districts additional resources—both goods and services—to help their community with teaching and learning. They simply need to appreciate the benefits of pursuing partnerships and become equipped to tap into a world of promising opportunities. This "how-to" book seeks to offer school leaders inclined toward entrepreneurialism the tools, including specific steps, for partnering with others so that they can bring to their schools unforeseeable and positive changes.

DESCRIPTION OF ENTREPRENEURIAL LEADERSHIP

The book is divided into two parts. Part I, which contains chapters 1 through 3, introduces ways in which K-12 administrators with entrepreneurial leadership characteristics can use the power of partnerships to support the needs of their schools and districts.

Chapter 1 provides an overview of entrepreneurial leadership, its importance in education, and its connection to forming partnerships in K-12 schools. A multiplicity of partnership benefits are described for students, parents, teachers, and administrators in relation to the educational experience.

Chapter 2 describes school-business, school-community, and school-college/university partnerships available to entrepreneurial leaders. This chapter discusses in detail reasons that motivate these three entities to partner with schools. Strategies and examples from the field on how to incentivize partners to form school partnerships are included.

Chapter 3 offers specific guidelines for entrepreneurial leaders to follow in building partnerships. This chapter identifies the challenges in schools that determine the types of partnerships to pursue. A variety of forms and checklists are included to help establish, implement, and evaluate partnerships.

Part II, which contains chapters 4 through 7, describes ways that entrepreneurial leaders have created pathways and can create pathways for partnerships with businesses, the community, and colleges and universities.

Chapter 4 concentrates on ways in which entrepreneurial leaders are developing partnerships with businesses. This chapter offers ideas and examples for using contacts and networks to connect with small, medium, and large businesses to bring services and resources to the schools. There is a focus on considerations, both pro and con, and guidelines for bringing businesses into the schools.

Chapter 5 focuses on forming school partnerships with community organizations and agencies. Pathways to connect with community organizations, identify their resources, tap into their goals, and develop a full-service community school are discussed. Included are many examples of potential community partners.

Chapter 6 explores the ways colleges and universities can partner with schools and school districts. The promises and challenges of three types of college/university partnerships are presented. The merits of a Professional Development School are examined.

Chapter 7 discusses critical components for successful partnerships, guidelines for sustaining partnerships, and considerations for renewing those partnerships that work. This chapter highlights the importance of entrepreneurial leadership and stakeholder satisfaction as key components for partnership longevity. Specific guidelines for sustaining partnerships end the chapter.

UNIQUE FEATURES OF ENTREPRENEURIAL LEADERSHIP

The chapters of this "how to" book contain practical ideas, real-life stories, step-by-step guidelines, and samples of documents to help create a blueprint for forging ahead with partnerships. Unique features include

- samples of checklists, inventories, partnership agreements, or assessment tools that can be adapted for a specific school or district;
- examples of entrepreneurial school and district leaders who have engaged in specific partnerships with information about these partnerships;
- real-life vignettes of individuals and groups from K-12 schools, businesses, communities, and colleges and universities who have embarked on a partnership and the steps taken to form such a partnership; and
- profiles of different school leaders who speak about their own entrepreneurial experiences with partnerships.

INTENDED OUTCOMES OF ENTREPRENEURIAL LEADERSHIP

As the entrepreneurial leaders in this book shared repeatedly, they knew that they had to go outside their four walls if they were going to be able to get the resources that their schools needed. These K-12 administrators believe that entrepreneurism is an important leadership quality that separates good leaders from bad ones. They believe that entrepreneurial leadership is all about organizing and motivating stakeholders to achieve the common goal of helping students achieve in an atmosphere that is conducive to growth.

The leaders in this book have discovered the many ways in which partnerships have changed the trajectory of their schools, and hope that others come to realize the same. We hope that after reading this book you too come to realize the importance of entrepreneurial leadership in K-12 education, assess and develop your own talents and skills for entrepreneurial leadership, and embark on the daunting and rewarding journey of launching partnerships that uplift your institutions in unprecedented ways.

Part I

ENTREPRENEURISM AND PARTNERSHIPS

Part I introduces ways in which K-12 administrators with entrepreneurial leadership characteristics can use the power of partnerships to support the needs of their schools and districts. Specific ways in which partnerships can benefit students, parents, teachers, and administrators are discussed in relation to existing research. Partnerships with businesses, community, and colleges and universities are described for their value in working with schools and their motivation for doing so. Guidelines that entrepreneurial leaders have used and can use to build such partnerships, from identifying challenges to creating a blueprint for implementation and evaluation, complete this first part of the book.

Chapter 1

Entrepreneurial Recognition of Partnership Opportunities

- *Middle school principal Harvey Bonmark declined an offer by a local corporation to begin an after-school business club for his students that would be organized by the corporation's employees.*
- *Middle school principal James Livestock quickly said that he wanted to pursue an offer by the same local corporation to begin the same type of after-school business club.*

Why did one principal say "yes" and one say "no" to the same partnership offer? The principals, both long-term educators in the district, are responsible for schools of comparable size with similar socioeconomic, racial, and academic profiles. They supervise teachers with similar union proclivities and have the same pressures to demonstrate success on statewide tests.

Principal Bonmark is satisfied with the status quo, and Principal Livestock is not. Principal Bonmark did not see anything useful in creating a business club for his students because he would prefer that his students continue with the same after-school activities that his students have been doing since his tenure ten years ago. He is not interested in the complications and challenges that could potentially arise with a partnership with a business that he perceives to be disingenuous in their outreach as do-gooders.

Principal Livestock, on the other hand, thinks that it is worth the effort with his teachers and parents to expose his students to people and practices in the business world. He is not as concerned about the quid pro quo of a partnership because he knows that he will not agree to anything that would jeopardize his school community. He sees this partnership as a chance to use an important local resource to help his students learn about careers in business and thinks that this club could be the impetus for developing other career-oriented clubs.

A major reason for the differences in the way the two principals responded is their *entrepreneurial* spirit for developing partnerships with external groups and organizations. Forming such a partnership requires that an administrator expend additional time, coordinate and collaborate with essential stakeholders, take calculated risks, and think differently about existing programming. It requires an administrator to embody entrepreneurialism.

CHARACTERISTICS AND EVOLUTION OF ENTREPRENEURIAL LEADERS

The concept of entrepreneurial leadership emerged from business as a way to address increased uncertainty and competitive pressure in the marketplace. Initially, the role of the entrepreneur, which dates back to the 1940s, focused on small business owners (Vesper & Gartner, 1997). At the turn of the twenty-first century, entrepreneurial leaders for large business organizations became vital because such individuals had the know-how and wherewithal to pursue opportunities faster and more advantageously than others (McGrath & MacMillan, 2000).

Early research on entrepreneurial leaders focused on their traits. Brockhaus and Horwitz (1986) determined that there are four major personality traits of entrepreneurs: need for achievement, internal locus of control, high risk-taking propensity, and tolerance for ambiguity. As late as 2010, there were claims of an entrepreneurial gene (Mount, 2010).

Contrasting research of entrepreneurial leaders has revealed that they have a mindset for pursuing opportunities and use a set of methods or practices that enable them to positively impact their organizations. Entrepreneurial leadership is no longer thought of as just a trait for a select few but rather a methodology that can be taught to many leaders (Neck, Greene, & Brush, 2014; Venkataraman, Sarasvathy, Dew, & Forster, 2012).

This new understanding has enabled large businesses to develop entrepreneurialism in their senior leaders. Such training has helped senior leaders take the initiative, be creative, manage risk rather than minimize it, and make business decisions. They are better able to identify opportunities, determine how these opportunities are beneficial for their customers, communicate clearly, coherently, and convincingly how these opportunities improve their organization's value, and take responsibility for pursuing such opportunities. As a result, they have achieved better bottom lines for their groups within their organizations (Roebuck, 2011).

ENTREPRENEURIAL LEADERSHIP IN K-12 SCHOOLS

Leaders in general have the ability to motivate, influence, and lead people toward a common goal or purpose (Balakrishnan, 2015). Entrepreneurial leaders see and seize opportunities. They see the world as open to a host of possibilities, pursue them with a variety of stakeholders, and know how to accept and leverage failure. Such leaders do not start with a predetermined goal, but rather allow opportunities to emerge (Sarasvathy, n.d.). They do not need perfect solutions but look for good-enough ones. Entrepreneurial leaders learn through action. They make right turns and wrong turns, and learn more about the right direction as they go (Schlesinger, Kiefer, & Brown, 2012).

While the concept of entrepreneurial leadership has its roots in the business world, it has recently received attention in the education world to steer schools to new heights. These efforts to improve school leadership are coming from the government, communities, and observers of education who believe that American education is lacking in comparison with other developed countries (Lynch, 2016a, 2018). Although school leaders do not have to focus on the amount of money that they bring in each day, they do have to focus on measurable achievement outcomes for their students.

RATIONALE FOR ENTREPRENEURIAL LEADERSHIP IN K-12 SCHOOLS

School leaders must concern themselves with budget allocations in relation to required and desired expenses. They need to make sure that they can provide the instructional services and extracurricular opportunities that their students need and ensure that their teaching staff are equipped to provide such services and opportunities. School leaders also need to differentiate the types of services that they can provide to accommodate the diverse needs of the students they are responsible for educating, whether it is students with special needs, students with non-English speaking backgrounds, or students from impoverished backgrounds.

Often, and unfortunately, the financial and personnel resources available to school leaders to accommodate the many needs in a school or district fall short. Or, the resources available simply are not as exciting, helpful, intriguing, and innovative as they might be. Those school leaders who realize that their students, teachers, parents, and community could have abundantly more fruitful opportunities to grow and learn as a result of reaching beyond their own borders have an entrepreneurial spirit for seeking new ventures with unpredictable, yet exciting possibilities.

Part of this innovative orientation is the ability to create and sustain dynamic partnerships, which could include acting as an informal project manager and advisor to such partnerships. Johns Hopkins University has created an online program for school leaders on entrepreneurism.

This program helps school leaders understand the theory and practice of such leadership in today's schools, and appreciate the importance of partnerships as a significant enterprise for developing K-12 schools more fully. Such programs help school leaders think outside the traditional institutional box and take risks to transform education (Davis & Molnar, 2014). See http://education.jhu.edu/academics/doctoral-programs/doctor-of-education/entrepreneurial-leadership-education/.

EXAMPLES OF ENTREPRENEURIAL LEADERSHIP PARTNERSHIP PURSUITS IN K-12 SCHOOLS

School leaders with entrepreneurial talents and skills (Hentschke, 2009) know how to capitalize on various partnership opportunities, which can involve businesses, communities, and college/universities. Partnerships can be as simple as the formation of an after-school tutoring club for second graders created by a faculty member from a local college or as complex as a university takeover of a school. A middle school principal in Los Angeles, California realized that only about 1 percent of his eighth-grade students were testing at grade level in mathematics.

This principal was dependent on long-term substitute teachers because he could not attract teachers to work in his school, which was one of the lowest performing schools in Los Angeles Unified School District. The University of California at Los Angeles (UCLA) formed a partnership with the school, which is now called the Horace Mann UCLA Community School. The new eighth-grade math teacher is on the faculty of UCLA's Graduate School of Education, the sixth-grade teacher is a UCLA doctoral student, and undergraduate students are tutoring the middle-school students. UCLA is benefitting from its ability to have its own faculty and students immersed in the school (Phillips & Kohli, 2016).

An elementary school principal in Saint Louis, Missouri formed a partnership with a local business. About 5 percent of her students are homeless and living in shelters. Unlike most of the other students in her school, these homeless children do not have access to computers and cannot complete many of the assignments. She reached out to a local electronics store to see if management would be willing to give out loaners to these children. In return, she would publicize the generosity of the store to her school community to help promote good will with this local business. The store manager was happy to oblige and, together, they developed a partnership agreement that satisfied both organizations.

The "Reading Friends" initiative in St. Croix Falls Elementary School in Wisconsin represents a school-community partnership that actually was initiated by a community member who wanted to bolster literacy. With the blessing of the school principal, the library media specialist coordinates the program with the community leader to assign volunteers, mostly senior citizens, to the classrooms of this rural school where more than 40 percent of the students receive free or reduced lunch.

In pre-K through first-grade classrooms, a dedicated volunteer spends an hour or more weekly with a student reading aloud or listening to the student read. In second through fourth grade, students are paired with a "Friend" for fifteen- to twenty-minute sessions weekly (Platt & Brissett-Kruger, 2015). This type of school-community partnership represents a principal's positive response to an idea from a community leader who communicated to teachers that if they opened their classrooms to outsiders, their students would benefit greatly.

When partnerships provide mutually beneficial opportunities, whether short-term or long-term, they enrich the lives of those involved and the culture of the organization in unanticipated ways. Entrepreneurial school leaders can bring to their schools and district additional resources—both goods and services—to help their community with teaching and learning. They simply need to appreciate the benefits of pursuing partnerships and tap into a world of promising opportunities for strengthening their schools.

Ray Sanchez, Superintendent of Ossining Union Free School District in New York, knows how to work creatively and diplomatically with employees, families, and the community to move forward his agenda of bringing resources to his schools. With his employees, he helps them to imagine and realize ideas to strengthen their efforts with their students. With his families, he participates in school- and district-based events so that they know that he is as committed as they are to attend functions that celebrate their children. With the community, he goes to where they are, whether it is churches, senior citizen homes, or village fairs to support and address their mutual concerns and celebrations.

Ray's success comes from his belief that nothing is impossible for his schools. As an entrepreneurial leader, he has quietly and subtly reached out to different university and community advocates to form partnerships that could benefit his teachers, students, and families. Not all of them have worked because of unanticipated financial glitches or personnel changes within his district or the partnership organizations. Nevertheless, Ray has used these experiences to reimagine other possibilities because, as an entrepreneur, he learns from his mistakes.

As the superintendent of an increasingly large Hispanic population, Ray has been involved with a local university to get support for his children, teachers, and parents through several initiatives. Ossining is organized according to the Princeton Plan so that all students in a specific grade within the district go to the same school. His school with all third and fourth graders is a Professional Development School. His principal and a university faculty member create engagement breakfasts for parents, reading and math nights for the entire family, and different types of professional development activities for the teachers.

He developed a program for his early childhood school so that teacher candidates could be hired into paid assistantship positions. These master's degree students served as teaching assistants in this early childhood school. He has his teachers involved in a parent committee at the university so that he can send large numbers of his parents to conferences, all in Spanish, focused on learning how to advocate for their own children's success. He has been so active and supportive that he even served as a keynote speaker for parents across the county, which speaks to his strong beliefs in parent education as well as his willingness to speak to a large audience.

Equally important to Ray is his desire to help his teachers develop professionally. He formed a partnership with a state-affiliated organization to encourage his teachers to seek advanced degrees in leadership. He then invited the state to visit his district so that he could showcase the types of partnership work in which his district was involved.

Ray exemplifies entrepreneurism and believes deeply in building partnerships within his community to foster educational success.

THE IMPORTANCE OF ENTREPRENEURIAL LEADERSHIP FOR FORMING PARTNERSHIPS

The formation of partnerships requires leaders who are willing to embark on the unknown. Partnerships could be considered professional marriages where two or more parties come together in good faith to try something new and different. They believe in each other but nevertheless are taking a chance that they will have a productive and fulfilling future. As with the union of two people, the signatories on partnership agreements understand that there are many more individuals who will be involved in contributing, or not, to the health and well-being of the relationship.

Some will be enthusiastically supportive of the partnership's mission and opportunities while others will vociferously resist the leaders' efforts to implement any aspect of it. This is where Schlesinger, Kiefer, and Brown

(2012)'s study of the success of entrepreneurial leaders helps. Rather than worrying about getting everyone's approval, leaders involve the people they know are supportive and committed to the partnership.

They take small steps, produce early results no matter how small, and manage expectations of what can be accomplished. If the partnership is not working as anticipated, they are not afraid to walk away. As with the institution of marriage, the success of a partnership depends on *mutual satisfaction* and *compromise*. If this is not possible, it is better to abort than persist with a disheartening situation.

A principal of an elementary school in Austin, Texas began a partnership with a nearby bookstore to encourage his second- and third-grade students to participate in activities and events that would excite them about reading. He felt that the iPad was dominating his young students' free time and wanted to help his parents motivate their children to read books for pleasure. The bookstore owner was appreciative because of his desire to attract more children to buy books.

Harry created a partnership agreement with the bookstore owner to cosponsor four thematic evening events: mystery, adventure, sports, and creative arts. Harry had the school librarian work with the bookstore owner to identify books for each theme that the second- and third-grade children could select. Part of the partnership agreement required that the bookstore owner work with adolescent and adult actors, musicians, athletes, dancers, and other community members to produce dramatic productions and create engaging activities for each of the special evenings, which would take place at the school for the children and their parents.

The bookstore owner agreed to pay for each event's personnel costs, and Harry agreed to pay for the equipment, materials, and supplies. The school's PTA agreed to subsidize the cost of books that the children purchased from the bookstore. The second- and third-grade teachers agreed to create projects, assignments, and informal assessments related to each set of books for their grade.

When the families came for "mystery" night, they discovered that the bookstore owner did not deliver what he had promised. The teachers had to step in last minute to engage the families in activities related to the books. Harry realized a bit too late that, while the bookstore owner had sponsored similar types of events in his store, which had given Harry the idea in the first place, the owner had overestimated his ability to plan for so many children and their parents.

Harry has since found a bookstore that, while not in the neighborhood, already had a successful history of working with schools. The dramatic productions have been top notch and the creative activities have motivated the children and their parents to prepare for their evening adventures.

Harry did not let one partnership failure stop him from moving onto another that would yield positive results. He used the lessons learned to find a partner who could deliver. He persisted in identifying pathways for enriching his children's educational experiences. He identified what he wanted, acknowledged that he could not deliver this on his own, and set out to find a partner who had the wherewithal, experiences, and resources to provide a spectacular program for all.

Textbox 1.1 provides a checklist of ten characteristics of an entrepreneurial leader. Use the checklist to determine if you are oriented to entrepreneurism. If you possess such qualities, it does not preclude you from having other leadership styles and characteristics. It simply means that part of your leadership profile includes qualities that enable you to reach out beyond your own school borders.

TEXTBOX 1.1   ENTREPRENEURIAL LEADERSHIP CHARACTERISTICS

Directions: Put a check next to any of the ten entrepreneurial characteristics. If you have checked at least half of the characteristics, you most likely possess entrepreneurial leadership characteristics.

- Pursues opportunities
- Takes calculated risks
- Makes difficult decisions and stands by them
- Provides essential stakeholders with a convincing rationale for pursuing opportunities
- Works creatively and diplomatically with essential stakeholders to bring out their best
- Self-regulates one's own emotions and is attuned to others' emotions
- Remains true to one's own aspirations in the face of opposition
- Tolerates ambiguity
- Accepts and leverages failure
- Learns through action, adjusts accordingly, and perseveres

DEFINITION AND BENEFITS OF PARTNERSHIPS

Partnerships are relationships. They are two or more people or organizations involved in the same activity, two or more people or groups working together for a common cause, or an organization formed by two or more people or groups working together for some purpose. They often involve a formal, written agreement that describes the purpose of the partnership and responsibilities of each of the parties involved (Hopkins, 2011).

Partnerships in education usually involve school districts with businesses, colleges/universities, and community organizations to help with student achievement, professional development, and administrative needs (Wepner, 2014). The benefits of partnerships are many. Partnerships allow ideas to expand. An excitement emerges when individuals come together and discover that they have similar goals and passionate opinions. As you listen to their suggestions and reflect on possibilities, you begin to realize how much more productive a group is even at the initial stage of discussion.

Partnerships reach more people and have greater impact than one individual or one institution can accomplish. They can provide the political clout needed to initiate change within a school or district. Partnerships help to get things done. They can generate enthusiasm and give individuals collective hope that a shared goal can be reached (Hopkins, 2011). Partnerships create opportunities for innovation, help to marshal resources, support a school's mission, and encourage calculated risk-taking.

Middle school principal James Livestock from the opening example recognizes that a partnership with a local corporation allows him to do something innovative for his students that he had not thought about previously. He knows that there are some risks involved in bringing in outsiders and anticipates some complications with student participation and parent approval, yet still believes that these are calculated risks that can be addressed as the partnership unfolds. Since he does not have a staff person in his school who has both the expertise and time to devote to developing such a club, he will be able to use the personnel that the corporation provides to offer this exciting opportunity to his students.

His school already runs other after-school programs so he does not have to worry about the necessary custodial or administrative services required for after-school programs. He believes that such a business club supports his school's mission of preparing students to be career and college-ready and hopes that eventually he can use the corporate volunteers to work alongside some of his parents and community supporters to present at career fair days.

Benefits for Students and Parents

Partnerships provide a variety of benefits for students and parents, which can include cost-free tutoring and learning experiences, parent engagement initiatives, free health care services, and exposure to college and career opportunities.

Cost-Free Tutoring and Learning Experiences. Cost-free tutoring can come from college/universities, businesses, and the community. Tutoring can be with individual students or small groups of students before, during, or after school. They can occur on weekends and during the summer. Tutoring can help with a range of learners; from those struggling to those interested in enrichment.

Universities are fertile ground for getting tutors for students. Undergraduate and graduate students in teacher education programs need time in schools to fulfill their academic and certification requirements. There also are students from other academic areas who are involved in clubs and organizations that promote tutoring in schools.

An adult teacher education student began an after-school, small-group tutoring club for middle school students struggling in math. Ten years later, this club is still in existence because the students who have participated voluntarily have shown remarkably improved scores on the statewide test.

Exciting learning experiences also come from different types of partnerships. A group of university students majoring in environmental science took their study of monarch butterflies to fifth-grade classrooms in one school. Rather than take the usual end-of-semester final, students opted to create a project that enabled the fifth graders to launch their own experiment about the monarch butterflies' flight patterns. The university students spent one day each week for most of the semester in the fifth-grade classrooms. The fifth-grade students were captivated by this experience, and the three fifth-grade teachers declared that this experience was far better than any that they could provide.

A huge flood in Cedar Rapids, Iowa in 2008 that devastated the city was the impetus for school-community partnership that created a unique learning opportunity for high school students. The local newspaper reached out to a high school STEM teacher to figure out ways to rebuild the community. This high school teacher sparked interest in the community to consider the idea of having a school without grades or classes. Rather than have students' learning measured by standardized tests, students could engage in project-based learning that would be evaluated by community partners.

Students, whether high achievers or nontraditional learners, pursue projects with teachers and community members that are used for traditional high school credit. For example, one student with an interest in the refugee crisis wrote a social studies curriculum around this issue and used a statistics course that she took to analyze data related to her refugee project. Called Iowa BIG, and as one principal shared, this partnership is helping to reimagine how to incorporate personalized, community-driven projects into the curriculum. Three schools have partnered to send their students and contribute their full-time employees to a separate site (Schwartz, 2018).

Parent Engagement Initiatives. Mary Foster, Assistant Superintendent of Peekskill School District in Peekskill, New York, knew about Manhattanville College's network of professional development schools that focused on the increase of Hispanic students in changing suburban schools. A Professional Development School (PDS) is an actual P-12 school that forms a partnership with a professional education program at a university. These schools, often considered innovative institutions, have a four-fold mission of preparing new teachers, providing professional development for currently practicing teachers, promoting collaborative inquiry, and helping with P-12 student learning.

Mary wanted her district to join the network so that her students could benefit from the services offered. Once a partnership agreement was signed to have her primary school of K-1 children from across the district become a PDS, she worked with the college to hire Felix Flores, a retired principal to serve as the liaison between the school and the university.

Felix has been intent on promoting parental involvement. He, with the support of the school administration, established a PDS Leadership Team to develop workshops and events for parents, which have been very well attended. These have focused on:

- Extending Learning at Home
- Managing Your Child
- Advocating for Your Child
- Extending and Continuing Learning through the Summer.

A core group of parent leaders has emerged in the school and district. Part of Felix's continued support of their leadership is his encouragement to attend the Hispanic Parent Leadership conferences that are held at the college. These conferences help parents to understand their role in supporting their children's language and literacy development as well as their physical and mental health habits. One of the two leadership conferences each year emphasizes ways to help children with special learning needs succeed in school.

Free Health Care Services. Free medical, dental, psychological, and counseling services are becoming more prevalent in schools that have deep and far-reaching relationships with community organizations. Principals often turn their schools into community schools to form multiple partnerships with different community organizations so that services are available to their students and families throughout the day, week, and even weekends (Coalition of Community Schools, 2016). School leaders recognize that they can capitalize on the good will of community partners for services that are especially important for families new to the United States with poverty, academic, and language challenges.

An example of an organization in the New York area that partners with schools to help parents with their children's nutritional health is Better Beginnings (Better Beginnings, 2016). This community organization engages parents of preschoolers in a series of interactive workshops about healthy eating habits. A school that partners with this organization is able to provide parents with free workshops. Parents learn about their own susceptibility to chronic disease, nutrition basics, ways to establish smart goals for their young children's eating, feeding practices, and ideas for creating a healthy home environment.

When parents complete these group sessions, which can be offered in English or Spanish, they receive a certificate of completion. As with this special program, there are humanitarian leaders in communities everywhere who want to bring their special programs and projects into the schools to help children and their families.

Exposure to College and Career Opportunities. Students as young as first grade can be introduced to the life and value of a university through partnership initiatives. Manhattanville College's PDS network of sixteen schools across eight school districts has as an expectation that all students in at least one grade level will visit the college each year. All expenses, including bus service and lunch, come from PDS funds. Each school develops its own activities, from a scavenger hunt at the college to an essay about the meaning of college, based on the age of the students and ways in which the college visit supports the curriculum.

College representatives from admissions, academic services, and student services meet with the students to enlighten them about various facets of college. The students take a campus tour, occasionally visit college classes, participate in activities developed by college students, and enjoy lunch in the college's castle. This type of learning experience is particularly enlightening for those students who would be the first in their families to attend college.

University coursework or programs for university credit can be very helpful to high school students. One program that some school district superintendents have adopted is the Cambridge Assessment International Education model, which competes with the Advanced Placement and International Baccalaureate programs. School administrators who have partnered with Cambridge pay a registration fee and annual membership dues to have access to online materials and training for teachers so that students can work with an outsourced curriculum that is focused on critical thinking and problem solving. There is also a charge for each exam.

High school students can take exams in various subjects to earn a Cambridge diploma credential. While currently most prevalent in Florida, there are concentrations of Cambridge schools in other states as well. This program from the United Kingdom believes that its focus on analysis, especially as expressed through writing, can help with students' college readiness (Adams, 2013; Sawchuck, 2018).

Some high schools look to partner with their local universities to offer courses that they simply cannot provide. A school district superintendent knew that he needed to do something for his students with advanced math skills because he simply did not have the budget to hire another math teacher. He created a partnership with a local university that enabled his students to take advanced mathematics courses with undergraduate students. These students were able to enroll in the courses tuition free because the high school was a PDS with the university. Part of the partnership agreement included vouchers for courses.

Benefits for Teachers and Administrators

When structured for the needs and interests of teachers and administrators, partnerships can provide cost-free assistance, professional development, curriculum development, and access to personnel and funding.

Cost-Free Assistance. Every teacher can benefit from additional assistance in the classroom. Of course, those assisting in classrooms need to be vetted for their intellectual capabilities, teaching skills and potential, psychological soundness, and moral compass. Once cleared, they offer unlimited opportunities for assisting teachers with students, whether it is with their assignments, content and skill acquisition, or social and emotional development.

Businesses often are motivated to increase volunteerism. In addition to serving as tutors, as noted in the previous section, business employees can serve as general volunteers for large group activities; for example, combined classes in technology labs in a secondary school. Community organizations with missions to bolster literacy or minimize bullying can have groups of volunteers ready to go into schools at varying times during the week to work with students.

University students can serve as apprentice instructors where they first shadow teachers and then teach lessons to K-12 students. They can help to implement data-driven instruction, enliven lessons with new strategies that they learned in university classrooms, and conduct small-group, follow-up lessons of concepts taught during whole-class instruction.

Professional Development. A major purpose of partnerships is to provide for teachers' professional development. Every teacher can benefit from learning something new; whether it is a new teaching strategy, another approach to work with students with learning challenges, innovative facets of the curriculum, recently published materials, or revised districtwide, state, or national standards. Partnerships contribute to teachers' renewal. They can stimulate collaborative inquiry, offer innovative and cutting-edge ideas, and raise the level of teacher expectation (Gilles, Wilson & Elias, 2009; Hamel & Ryken, 2010).

Teachers might be invited to make presentations with their partners at local, state, national, and even international conferences because of the work that they are doing in their classrooms. A favorite for teachers are Lunch & Learns, Brunch & Learns, Book Clubs, and Study Groups because they stem from teachers' interests and are informal, friendly gatherings at teachers' convenience. A few popular topics could include culturally relevant pedagogy, reading and writing workshop, responsive classrooms, questioning strategies, and teaching assistants' roles. Often, teachers co-host these small-group learning opportunities because they have developed expertise that needs to be shared.

Book clubs often focus on newly published books for children and adolescents or self-help books for professionals. A favorite book of one study group was *Grit: The Power of Passion and Perseverance* by Angela Duckworth (2016) because it helped the teachers to think about ways to persevere with their most challenging students and disengaged families.

Staff development workshops hosted by partners also offer rich professional development opportunities when focused on *relevant* topics. These can be offered to small groups of interested teachers across grade levels or by grade level, or to the entire staff. An individual, a team, or a panel can conduct these workshops. Topics can focus on curricular revisions, new assessment options, implementation of a dual language program, or technology safety measures with new electronic tools.

These professional development opportunities refresh teachers' repertoire of conceptualizations, methodologies, and strategies. However, they do not necessarily *transform* teachers' instruction. It is not about problems with the purpose, content, or format, but rather about the lack of frequency and intensity. For teachers to truly change their teaching patterns and styles, they need to be steeped in learning through one-on-one or small-group mentoring over extended periods of time.

When schools are fortunate to have partnerships with deep pockets for funding such mentoring, they most probably will see significant changes in teachers' development. Some schools in Westchester County, New York have had this good fortune because of a partnership with an Institute that had funding from a donor. Teachers received a yearlong, job-embedded mentoring opportunity on a multisensory, phonics-based approach to reading that advanced the foundational literacy skills of early readers by improving the instructional expertise of teachers.

The principals recognized such a need in their K-2 teachers, reached out to the Institute, and created a partnership for this purpose. Principals can find seriously effective mentoring opportunities with different types of partnership organizations. A great example is a principal from Pennsylvania who was determined to have her technologically phobic teachers learn to use and infuse technology into their teaching. This beloved principal spent years trying to convince her very talented teachers to experiment with one or two instructional programs. The teachers did not have the ability to do it.

This principal formed a partnership with a local university so that, together, they could apply for a state grant. They were fortunate to get the grant, which included both the hardware and the professional development. The local university's faculty and teacher candidates served as the yearlong mentors for the teachers. By the end of the year, these once-reluctant teachers were using technology in their daily teaching. They needed frequent and consistent instruction, guidance, and support, which the university faculty and students were able to provide.

Curriculum Development. Assistance with the curriculum can come from university faculty, community experts, and business professionals. A great example of a principal who formed a partnership with a business to enhance the curriculum is Melanie Welsh from Reseda Charter High School in Reseda, California. She formed a partnership with Amgen Biotech Experience (ABE) to provide an innovative science education program.

This program empowers teachers to bring biotechnology to their classrooms. ABE features a hands-on molecular biology curriculum designed to introduce students to the excitement of scientific discovery. This program provides teacher professional development, curriculum materials, and research-grade equipment and supplies to secondary schools at no cost.

Substitute Teachers. A shortage of available and qualified substitute teachers often plagues many building principals, especially during flu and holiday seasons when teachers are more likely to be absent from school. The state in which your school resides can contribute to or hinder your ability to find substitute teachers. While some states are lenient with qualifications, and only require an associate degree or even a high-school diploma, most states do require that a substitute teacher has a bachelor's degree.

Suburban and rural school districts often are challenged with their available pool of substitute teachers because they might not be able to rely on substitute teaching agencies the way some city school districts do. For instance, any substitute teacher for the Philadelphia City School District must apply through Kelly Educational Staffing® to get a position.

Universities with education programs can provide substitute teachers. An assistant superintendent in charge of personnel discovered this resource. She formed a partnership with her local university to create an internship program that enabled students ready for student teaching to spend half of the year as an unpaid student teacher and half of the year as a paid substitute teacher. A variation of the intern concept has since evolved to provide in-house substitute teachers. School administrators form partnerships with local universities to offer teacher candidates yearlong contracts to serve as both substitute teachers and learners in the classroom.

Such contracts specify the maximum number of hours per week that teacher candidates can work as substitute teachers and usually elaborate on the type of work that can occur as learners (e.g., lesson/unit development, tutoring, and attendance at faculty meetings). Although these contracts are between the district and teacher candidate, universities use their marketing engines and faculty capital to promote these programs.

Funding. Partnerships can be a great source of funding for projects, materials, and even personnel. A business-school partnership between a Texas-based investment group, Capital North, and a middle school provides office supplies for teachers, school supplies for students, and funds for field trips. A start-up tech company that wanted to field-test a product created a partnership with an elementary school so that each fifth-grade student could receive an electronic pen to use for their assignments. A philanthropist intent on helping teachers to improve their teaching methodologies formed a partnership with an elementary school to fund each primary teacher's yearlong professional development activities (Northside Independent School District, 2015).

Now that you have read about some of the benefits of partnerships, see how many of the ten reasons for possibly pursuing partnerships in Table 1.1 resonate with you.

Table 1.1 Beliefs in Partnerships

I BELIEVE that	Yes	No	Uncertain
Partnerships can offer new opportunities to my school/district.			
Partnerships can infuse new blood into building.			
Partnerships can help to solve problems.			
Potential partners can provide assistance to teachers, students, parents, and administrators.			
Partnerships can improve student-teacher ratios.			
Partnerships can stimulate collaborative inquiry.			
Roadblocks for forming partnerships can be overcome.			
Partnerships can enrich the way my teachers think.			
Partnerships can provide the political clout needed to initiate change within a school or district.			
First steps can be taken to pursue and establish a partnership with a promising partner.			

Directions: Review each of the ten statements. Check "Yes" if you agree with the statement, "No" if you do not agree, and "Uncertain" if you are not yet convinced that the statement is accurate. If you have checked "Yes" to at least half of the statements, you are leaning toward appreciating the value of partnerships.

PARTNERSHIPS, ENTREPRENEURIAL REQUIREMENTS, AND THE EDUCATIONAL EXPERIENCE

Partnerships require give and take from all stakeholders. Even the most supportive members of a partnership might find it difficult to accept ideas from others or give up ideas about which they are passionate. Those responsible for developing partnerships need to cultivate compromise, help cut through the red tape, get commitment from all parties, and help everyone feel they have equal voice that can at times impede progress (Hopkins, 2011).

Leaders who develop and implement partnerships need to have courage and patience to deal with obstacles throughout the process. They must have the capacity to encourage, compliment, inform, rethink, cajole, consider, and adjust (Hopkins, 2011). They must be vigilant, visible, and respectful. They must keep their eye on the ball because they know that when partnerships become available they have the potential to augment realities.

Principal Bonmark from the opening paragraph knew enough about himself to say "no" to the local corporation to begin an after-school business club. He did not have the interest or wherewithal to engage in the process of forming this partnership. He justified his decision by criticizing this partner's intent. Unfortunately, his students could lose out on something potentially valuable.

Principal Livestock interpreted the partnership offer entirely differently. He saw this overture as an opportunity to provide something worthwhile for his students that could be the beginning of something exciting in his school. He was eager to work with his stakeholders to bring this local business into his school. Although he might not have been prepared for the unanticipated twists and turns of developing and sustaining such a partnership, he was willing to take the necessary risk to move forward.

He was confident enough in his own negotiating skills that he knew he would not compromise his school in any way. His belief in the partnership's potential for taking his school to the next level drove his enthusiasm for getting started, even with the many potentially challenging exchanges facing him. Principal Livestock exemplifies entrepreneurism.

As with any K-12 entrepreneur, Principal Livestock will have to do the following as he moves forward:

- be patient with his stakeholders and his own progress
- self-check his own behaviors and attitudes
- enjoy his mini achievements in forming this partnership
- see hiccups as opportunities and not deal-breakers
- keep his eye on the ball.

Chances are that Principal Livestock will do just fine because he is oriented to imagine possibilities as he capitalizes on opportunities. In contrast, Principal Bonmark appears quite satisfied with what exists, and is not interested in pursuing what seems to be unnecessary. Some researchers would say that Principal Bonmark does not have the essential characteristics to form partnerships because he does not think entrepreneurially.

Others would claim that if Principal Bonmark could begin to appreciate the advantages of pursuing opportunities rather than holding onto the status quo, he could be taught specific methodologies that would enable him to pursue partnerships and other interesting initiatives. Recent research about entrepreneurism has led to the belief that leaders can learn certain entrepreneurial techniques if they believe that their students will benefit. Their immediate response to opportunities might not be a visceral excitement, but they can and will entertain ideas if the right data are presented.

The Principal Bonmarks will not want to prevent students, teachers, and parents from benefitting from the "extras" that come with partnerships. As this chapter has shared, partnerships enable students to have "reading friends," new curricular offerings, tutoring in a variety of subjects, helping hands, mentors, scholarship opportunities, exposure to new clubs, and exciting learning experiences. Partnerships enable teachers to have additional help, resources, and professional development, and enable parents to have additional attention and resources.

Although these leaders might need others to coax them along or depend on other colleagues to be in the forefront of pursuing prospects and generating ideas, they will nevertheless not impede progress for their stakeholders. These slightly risk-averse leaders do, however, need to be convinced of the powerful influence of partnerships in their schools and districts. The chapters that follow provide the necessary steps for pursuing, developing, and sustaining such partnerships. As you read these chapters, think about what would help to convince the Principal Bonmarks to take the plunge.

Chapter 2

Partnership Types

- *Business:* Two low-income school districts, one in St Louis, Missouri, and the other in Fairfield, California, partnered with Whirlpool to mitigate absenteeism. Students were absent from school because they were teased and bullied. They did not have the resources to wash their clothes and would rather be absent than face the teasing and bullying about being unkempt and dirty. Whirlpool's Care Counts program donated a total of seventeen washers and dryers to the two districts. Students are able to wash and dry their clothes during school hours. The students feel proud wearing clean clothes; attendance, class participation, and motivation increased (Weller, 2016).
- *Community:* The Rotary Club of New Brunswick's (New Jersey) Dictionary Project puts special dictionaries that include teacher resources in the areas of history, science, and math in the hands of all third graders in three local elementary schools. The dictionaries are gifts the students can take home and keep to develop reading, writing, and thinking skills (New Brunswick Rotary Club, 2002–2019).
- *College/University:* The Phuture Phoenix Program of the University of Wisconsin-Green Bay partners with twenty-two elementary, middle, and high schools in Wisconsin. Through coordinated resources and mission, more than 1,400 students are tutored and mentored and given campus tours by more than 175 university students. The overall goal is to give underrepresented and disadvantaged students opportunities to experience academic success and realize that college is possible (American Association of State Colleges and Universities, n.d.).

A partnership, by definition, is a relationship between two or more parties. Successful partnerships are mutually beneficial relationships. All parties and stakeholders get something out of the relationship. One party initiates the partnership in order to secure a service or product, fulfill a need, or garner support in some fashion. Partners who work with schools often acknowledge that they share interest and responsibility to invest in children (Epstein, 2010).

The Interstate School Leaders Licensure Consortium (ISLLC) has developed standards for school leaders and through the standards has given a working definition of a school leader as someone "who promotes the success of all students by collaborating with families and community members, responding to diverse community interests and needs, and mobilizing community resources" (Murphy & Shipman, 1999, p. 218).

Hatch (2009) advocates that school leaders should create outside-inside connections:

> The challenges you face *inside* the school are connected to and compounded by the things that are happening *outside*. In fact, schools face a number of external demands and pressures that they have to address. Moreover, without the connections, support, and expertise that come from interacting with a host of people, organizations, and institutions on the outside, schools cannot develop the goals, staff, or productive work environment they need to be successful. (p. 16)

When initiating a partnership, entrepreneurial school leaders need to consider the possible benefits or WIIFMs—What's In It For Me? WIIFMs are incentives. In other words, what will partners gain from the partnership? How does this new partner's institution or group benefit from the school partnership? What would motivate the new partner to develop a relationship with our school or district? While exploring partnership possibilities and opportunities, school leaders need to help potential partners identify and articulate their WIIFMs as well as considering their own WIIFMs.

When both partners' WIIFMs match, both can see the benefits, both have buy-in, and a partnership can be formed.

MOTIVATION FOR PARTNERS TO GET INVOLVED IN SCHOOLS

What motivates organizations to become a partner in education? What are the WIIFMs? These are some of the questions school leaders need to think about when approaching a potential partner. Likewise, when approached by a business or community agency to form a partnership, the school leader needs to ask himself or herself similar questions. What will my school and community gain from the partnership? Do we have the capacity to participate in this partnership? Will my faculty, staff, students, and their families buy into the partnership?

Much depends on the type of organizations that want to partner with a school or school district. Each partnership has unique characteristics as they represent the meshing of needs and goals of the partners.

THREE TYPES OF PARTNERSHIPS

There are three basic types of entrepreneurial partnerships with schools: school-business partnerships, school-community partnerships, and school-college/university partnerships. School partnerships range in size from a relationship with one staff member or school leader to multiple relationships numbering in the hundreds that extend throughout the entire school district. Figure 2.1 displays the three types of partnerships with K-12 schools.

Businesses

There has been a growing trend of business-school partnerships. According to the Council for Corporate and School Partnerships, business-school partnerships increased 33 percent from 1991 to 2007 (Sloan, 2008). Business-school partnerships are defined as a relationship between a school or school district and a commercial, usually for profit, business or agency. The types of business–school partnerships range from an informal agreement between a teacher and a local employer to formal relationships with national employers and school districts (Sloan, 2008). Through business partnerships, entrepreneurial school leaders can receive donations in the form of money, goods, and/or services (Education World, 1996–2019).

Monetary donations can initiate and support school programs, activities, equipment, and scholarships. For example, many national restaurant chains support school fundraising by donating a percentage of the sales for a particular event (e.g., Applebee's, Boston Market, Buffalo Wild Wings, Chipotle, Friendly's, Panda Express, Panera Bread, Ponderosa Steakhouse, or TGI Friday's).

Potbelly Sandwich Shops have three fundraising options for schools. Schools can opt for a gift-card event, an in-restaurant event in which the school receives 25 percent of the sales, or a specially created milkshake event in honor of the school for which Potbelly donates fifty cents for each shake sold (McFadden, 2016).

Businesses can also support schools by donating their goods and products to the schools. At the local level, a community grocery store donates

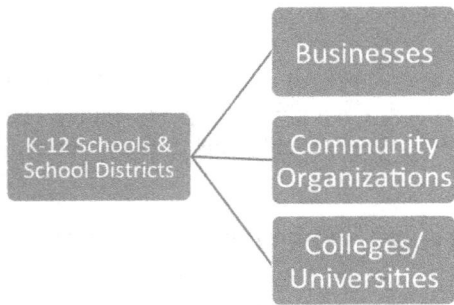

Figure 2.1 Types of Partnerships.

refreshments for a parent-teacher meeting or a pizza shop donates pizza for a classroom celebration. National businesses and corporations also donate goods.

Principal Akbar Cook from Newark, New Jersey, also purchased washing machines and dryers to combat absenteeism and bullying (see opening vignette). He did not participate in Whirlpool's Care Counts program. He applied for and received a grant from his state's electric utility foundation, Public Service Energy and Gas (PSEG), to pay for the appliances. He also partnered with a local United Parcel Service (UPS) that donated detergent and cleaning supplies to keep the project going.

Both programs, Whirlpool's Care Counts and PSEG Foundation/UPS, were a win-win. School leaders reported increased attendance rates, class participation, peer interaction, and motivation because students no longer felt embarrassed about wearing dirty clothes to school. The businesses received free publicity and tax breaks by helping students (Araujo, 2018; Weller, 2016).

A business or company might provide a service, rather than a product, as LEGO did with their international partnership with Montour School District in Montour, Pennsylvania. Montour was designing and creating a LEGO room in their building. LEGO in Denmark skyped with members of the district to advise them on the room's physical arrangement. While LEGO did not provide any pieces, they did provide advice and expertise (see Justin Aglio's vignette in chapter 4).

Communities

A school-community partnership is a relationship between a school or school district and a community of individuals or community agencies (Sanders & Lewis, 2005). School leaders can form partnerships with individual community members such as a local historian, clergy, school district alumni, and their own teachers. Local cultural, recreational, and social agencies are other resources for partnerships. Examples of local social agencies are Kiwanis and Rotary Clubs, some mental and medical health agencies, and youth development groups.

The entire community reaps benefits when schools and community organizations form partnerships to support student learning. Student academic achievement and success have been attributed to community partnerships focused on learning. One type of school-community partnership is the formation of after-school programs. After-school programs augment and complement school curricula, support concepts taught in school using different strategies and pedagogies, ease transitions from school to school (e.g., from elementary to middle school and from middle to high school), and give access to a variety of resources in the form of facilities, programs, and personnel (Little, 2013).

Providence After School Alliance (PASA) of Rhode Island partners with three area schools and coordinates a multitude of after-school programming to help schools improve student achievement. An area Title I school, Roger Williams, is one of PASA's partners. The staffing resources and funding allow Roger Williams' students a greater variety of programs for academic support and enrichment. More program options mean more students can participate. Roger Williams offers 45 different programs to more than 350 students. The program providers are individual community members, community organizations, and the local police department (Little, 2013).

The director of nonprofit OregonASK partnered with local schools to combat low-income students' loss of academic achievement and lack of daily nutritious meals during the summer months by using school libraries and federally funded summer programs. Most schools have libraries and most school libraries are generally closed during the summer months. Food is one of the few federally funded summer programs. OregonASK asked the school principals to keep their libraries open during the summer as a food site, thus providing reading activities and nutritional meals for students (Cline, 2018).

Colleges/Universities

Schools and school districts partner with colleges and universities to share resources and ideas. Partnerships can range from working with one university professor who has particular knowledge or a unique skill to participating in a network of fully developed professional development schools (PDSs) or full service community schools (see chapter 6 for PDS partnerships). Goods and products might be interchanged; however, it is more likely that the partnership shares ideas, resources, and services.

Dr. McNicholas-Bevensee, professor of biology at the University of Alabama at Birmingham, advocates for STEM and wants children to be responsible for their health. She developed the CDIB Science Outreach Program for elementary schools. The students rotate through five health stations monitored by university volunteers. What began as a partnership with one school, this program is now in four schools reaching more than 1,000 students (Royal, 2019).

Averell Elementary School's (Virginia) principal approached his PDS university partner about ongoing behavioral management problems occurring in his school. The professor gathered university colleagues and school leadership to provide professional development on classroom and behavior management. The partners used multiple-source, multiple-informant data to design professional development to meet the teachers' needs. Data were frequently shared with all stakeholders. As this partnership showed, targeted professional development plans, rather than commercial products, can help teachers improve their instruction (Hirsch, Ely, Lloyd, & Isley, 2018).

WHY BUSINESSES FORM PARTNERSHIPS WITH SCHOOLS

Businesses are vested in their communities as they want a strong workforce to work for them and consumers who will purchase their products (Alliance for Excellent Education, 2013). Schools provide resources for the workforce and educated consumers for their products. Businesses partner with schools because it helps them to invest in their community, stimulate interest in their products or services, and develop career-ready employees for the future.

Charles Katz, Director of Corporate Engagement at the National Academy Foundation suggested that partnerships with businesses support the 3Rs of rigor, relevance, and relationships (Alliance for Excellent Education, 2013). Bringing businesses into the schools connects curriculum with employment and careers. Curriculum becomes relevant and rigorous. Students learn about the importance of becoming career ready by earning a high school diploma and a college degree.

Students who engage with business employees learn about the competitive nature of business and the skills and dispositions necessary to work in the field. A school-business partnership provides the business with publicity in the surrounding community and possibly beyond the immediate area.

Workforce Competitiveness

Partnering with schools helps businesses to develop the type of workforce necessary to run their business. They have the opportunity to work with students so that they understand specific expectations for succeeding in different types of businesses. Businesses also have an entrée into schools to identify future talent, which helps them to remain competitive in their field.

Good Will

Business-school partnerships generate good will and potential consumer loyalty. A positive relationship between a school and business often results in partners seeking each other out for goods and services. For the business, good will brings positive returns in publicity and earnings.

Summer time presents a challenge for both parents and local movie theaters. Parents need activities to keep their children engaged and active. Movie theatres need to find a way to get patrons into the theaters. A mutually beneficial, though limited partnership, is one between local school districts and AMC Theaters' Summer Movie Camp. AMC's Summer Movie Camp offers a movie and a KidPack (popcorn, drink, and fruit snack) Wednesday mornings at 10:00 a.m. during the summer months.

AMC promotes the Movie Camp in the schools. AMC gets patrons into the theater during a slow season, establishes good will by providing a program that keeps children busy during the summer, and increases the potential for repeated attendance at their venue.

Good Publicity in the Surrounding Community

Publicity is a key component and a large portion of a business's operating budget. Partnering with a school gives a business the opportunity to advertise to parents, teachers, staff, and students, all of whom are consumers or potential consumers of their products or service. Caution about the impact of advertising in the schools is discussed in chapter 4.

The business partnership between Beanetic Coffee Roasters and Falls Church High School in Fairfax County, Virginia demonstrates why businesses seek partnerships with schools (Sloan, 2008). Beanetic wanted to counteract the predicted skill gap and workforce shortage to remain competitive in the coffee market. The school used the existing culinary arts class to help students learn all aspects of the coffee business, from growing to blending to marketing.

The school then worked with Beanetic to incorporate the coffee business into several school subject areas: the science of coffee roasting, history of coffee production, geography of where coffee grows, its effects on global economy, and the mathematics of percentages of types of beans to blend. The school culminated this project by having students develop and sell their own coffee blend, Jaguar Joe.

Beanetic found that partnering with the school improved the morale of its employees as they felt good about working with the students. The sale of

Jaguar Joe increased Beanetic's visibility in the community. It was a win-win for the school and the business.

WHY COMMUNITY ORGANIZATIONS FORM PARTNERSHIPS WITH SCHOOLS

Emily Keating, Director of Education for the Jacob Burns Film Center (JBFC) in Pleasantville, New York, actively seeks out partnerships with area school districts to bring JBFC's resources to the schools to teach literacy for a visual culture. This nonprofit organization's flagship program and curriculum, Image Sound and Story, is designed for classrooms, grades 3–12. JBFC offers professional development workshops to teachers to prepare and inspire them to implement digital media and visual storytelling into their English/Language Arts program (Grand Pré, 2017).

Students develop visual literacy by viewing and discussing media, capturing and editing images and video, and revising and reflecting on their work so that they are becoming visual storytellers. Teachers who commit to this program receive support from JBFC faculty in the classroom and through monthly community gatherings. Teachers also are eligible to have their students take a field trip to the JBFC campus to see and discuss films with JBFC faculty. Teachers from under-resourced schools can request funds from JBFC to pay for transportation and may participate in professional development free of charge.

Emily continually works at getting the word out about the various educational programs that JBFC offers. Many educators in the New York metropolitan region continue to be unfamiliar with JBFC's education mission, not realizing it is more than an art house for film screenings. JBFC aims to transform the definition of literacy in an age dominated by the visual image. They are a resource for the thoughtfully integrating technology and providing relevant and impactful literacy skills. Emily realizes her pitch needs to reach the ears of school leadership.

Currently, JBFC partners with more than 100 schools. Emily's partnerships with schools are successful because she deeply understands and respects the challenges schools face. From the outset, expectations are designed to be manageable, aspirational, and sustainable. Her goal is to have multiyear commitments between the JBFC and schools so that students across the grades can engage in this innovative visual literacy curriculum. Emily needs to get the word out and schools need to know that this resource exists.

Every school district is part of a community. The term community has been redefined through school-community partnerships. Community is "not only the neighborhoods where students' homes and schools are located but also any neighborhood that influences their learning and development" and includes "all who are interested in and affected by the quality of education, not just those with children in the schools" (Epstein, 2010, p. 86).

Traditional community organizations are usually located in the surrounding geographical area of the school. These organizations come in many shapes and sizes with often distinct missions or goals to serve the community in which they are located. Organizations that focus on health care, government and military, national service and volunteerism, faith, senior citizens, and culture and recreations are potential school-community partners (Sanders & Lewis, 2005). School-community partnerships can also be developed with individuals in the community.

Community Health

Most of these organizations are not-for-profits and have a mission to serve or support their community. They enter into partnerships with schools to fulfill their mission for the betterment of their communities. The mission of Open Door, a medical organization in Westchester and Putnam counties of New York, is about "keeping the people of Westchester and Putnam Counties healthy and strong, regardless of their ability to pay" (Open Door Family Medical Center and Foundation, n.d.a).

Open Door partners with local schools to provide free health and medical services in the school. In the school-based health centers, all students are eligible to receive care with only parental permission. Nurse practitioners are assigned to the schools to provide health services directly to the children onsite. In addition to responding to health needs as they arise, the nurse practitioners go into the classrooms to support programs in preventive and chronic care. They administer free flu shots, organize Smoke Free pledges, and supervise asthma support groups. These services help to reduce absenteeism and promote personal and academic success.

Open Door's partnerships with schools does not only fulfill its mission "to keep children healthy and in school" (Open Door Family Medical Center and Foundation, n.d.b). By locating their services in schools they solve a practical problem. The volume of patients/clients and physical space demands are reduced in their general health clinics (Lindsey Farrell, personal communication, October 10, 2018), which enables them to provide better services in both the clinics and the schools.

Community Well-Being

Community service organizations such as Girls Inc., Young Women/Young Men Christian Associations (YW/YMCA), the Rotary Club, Kiwanis Club, and Lions Club also partner with schools to contribute to the functionality and well-being of their communities. For example, Kiwanis strives to empower communities to improve the world by making lasting differences in children's lives (Kiwanis International, 2019). Partnerships with local schools are a logical fit for community organizations because they fulfill the needs of the organization and those of the schools.

Community organizations and agencies are not the only source of school-community partnerships. Individual members, acting as solo agents, can also develop partnerships with schools. The motivation of a single community member to develop a partnership with a school is usually for a personal and individual reason. It might be to share a talent, provide information, recruit members for a cause, develop a workforce, or promote a product.

Culture of Good Citizenship

Once a school-community partnership is established, its beneficial effects can ripple throughout the community. Home-school connections are promoted, volunteerism increases, and school-age children and youth become engaged in a larger community. Such connections develop a citizenship network in which all members of a community have a stake and ownership, which in turn can help develop a culture of community activism and safety.

A clear example of the effects of a school-community partnership that is benefiting entire communities is Partners for Student Success (PFSS) of St. Cloud, Minnesota. Founded on the principle that student success is a community issue, the core values of PFSS are:

- when students succeed, the entire community succeeds
- every student must be supported in and out of school
- learning encompasses more than just the traditional classroom
- data-driven decisions lead to better outcomes
- success for all students can only be achieved by a shared, voluntary, and clear commitment across the network partners (Partners for success, n.d.).

The PFSS network of more than seventy partnerships between St. Cloud's school districts and the area's businesses, educational institutions, community agencies, funders, and government satisfies the WIITFMs for all parties. The organizations within the PSFF network provide a wide spectrum of services such as:

- health care by CentraCare Health
- government and military
- City of St. Paul and Great River Regional Library

- national service and volunteerism—United Way, the Red Cross, and Girl Scouts
- faith by Catholic Charities
- culture and recreations—American Indian Center of Minnesota State University and Boys and Girls Clubs.

PFSS is constellation of groups working together to further the education of students from cradle to career while serving the needs and obligations of the individual organization (Partners for success, n.d.).

WHY COLLEGES AND UNIVERSITIES FORM PARTNERSHIPS WITH SCHOOLS

The American Association of State Colleges and Universities (AASCU) cites partnering with other educational institutions as one of three types of partnerships in which institutions of higher education (IHE) engage. Partnerships benefit IHEs by providing pathways to accomplish their missions, cultivate research and learning opportunities for faculty and students, and develop employment opportunities for their students and alumni (American Association of State Colleges and Universities, n.d.).

Colleges and universities need K-12 schools to help them honor the commitments they have to their students by providing sites to develop curriculum, conduct research, serve the community, engage in experiential learning, and receive and supervise interns and student teachers.

Preparation of New Teachers

Colleges and universities that have teacher education programs partner with local and area schools to support their teacher candidates. The clinical model, likened to medical students' experiences, is endorsed by the American Association of Colleges of Teacher Education (AACTE). This model is often a statewide requirement to provide real-life experiences to future teachers throughout their programs. These experiences take place in schools with real students, teachers, and administrators.

Manny Aceves is an associate dean of education at Loyola Marymount University (LMU) in Los Angeles, California. He views LMU's partnership with Los Angeles Unified School District as a new and necessary approach to teacher education. He believes that preparing teachers on campuses, devoid of *real* students is no longer viable. He purports that his university provides future educators with much stronger teacher preparation through on-site partnership experiences (Phillips & Kohli, 2016).

School-based, clinical-type experiences are usually designed to help teacher education candidates' progress gradually with increasingly more responsibilities in real-world classrooms. Commonly, school-based experiences begin with teacher candidates observing classes in action to working with a small group of students to teaching a mini lesson to an entire class and ultimately to student/intern teaching. These types of experiences model those of medical schools and are considered best practices in teacher preparation.

School-college/university partnerships facilitate the placement of teacher candidates and student teachers. The teachers and administrators in these schools and districts become partners in the education of future teachers. The college or university works with schools and districts to match the strengths and challenges of teacher candidates with particular schools or cooperating/mentor teachers.

Sites for Teaching College Courses

School-college/university partnerships help students and faculty. Students in teacher preparation programs benefit when college professors hold classes at partner schools. Such field-based courses create a laboratory model, which helps to bridge the theory to practice gap. Education professors' ability to have access to these classroom sites enables them to explain and demonstrate in real time critical elements of their course content.

Teacher candidates have the opportunity to experience the reality of current classroom environments. There is no need to use simulations, videos, or lectures to teach educational theory and methodology. Professors can bring their students into the classroom to witness theory in practice, discuss behavior management, model pedagogy, and demonstrate co-teaching.

Students in teacher preparation programs are not the only college/university students who benefit from school-college/university partnerships. Those studying a variety of other majors and fields also find the partnership experience enriching and beneficial. Partnership schools are convenient and provide easy access sites to satisfy course requirements, community service, and volunteerism. Mathematics and science majors can tutor K-12 students in after-school programs. Sociology and psychology students can observe student behavior. Athlete scholars can coach sports and help students develop good sportsmanship and physical education skills.

Research

College and university professors and administrators also benefit from K-12 partnerships when it comes to research. School-college/university partnerships are fertile ground for research and provide a setting to "ground research questions in real-world contexts" (Walsh & Backe, 2013, p. 605). Researchers can test out hypotheses and develop cutting-edge research about teaching and learning across a variety of disciplines.

College and university faculty need to conduct research and publish to be promoted in rank and tenured. For school of education faculty, schools are their laboratories. Dr. James, University of Georgia, and her graduate research assistant partnered with the principal, an art teacher, and a third grade teacher in one of Clarke County School District's professional development schools to investigate integrated curriculum to promote social and emotional growth through authentic collaborative inquiry (ACI) (James, Kobe, Shealey, Roretich, & Sabatini, 2015).

Over the course of a year the research partnership grew and they developed the *Head, Heart, Hand* project that integrated civic mindfulness, science, and art. University and school faculty benefited from the partnership. The team approach gave Dr. James access to students and teachers. It grounded her research in reality. Her presence in the school allowed her to expand her research to the national level. The experience also transformed the teachers' curriculum, teaching practices, and authorship (James et al., 2015). WIIFMs for all.

Professional development of university professors can take place at partnership school sites. Professors who are on site in schools have the opportunity to view issues and curriculum through a more practical lens than those professors who remain campus-bound. School-college/university partnerships are places where theory, research, and practice converge. The results are often enhanced pedagogy at the college/university level (Walsh & Backe, 2013).

Recruitment of Students and Faculty

Two potentially unexpected resources that emerge from college/university partnerships with schools are student recruitment and adjunct instructor recruitment. The University of Maryland's College of Engineering partners with middle and high schools of Delaware. Their Mechanical Engineering Student Squad (MESS) creates curriculum and then teaches it through hands-on engineering demonstrations. The main purpose of the department-wide program is to promote "recruitment, retention and advancement of young mechanical engineers" (University of Delaware, 2017).

Relationships develop between college/university faculty and administrators and school faculty and administrators who participate in partnerships. Faculty from both types of institutions work together, side by side in the K-12 partnership schools, and get to know about interests, areas of expertise, and teaching style. These relationships can lead to identifying a pool of potential course instructors for the college/university.

Manhattanville College in Purchase, New York has a partnership in the form of a professional development school (PDS) with Thomas A. Edison elementary school. The PDS has been in existence for more than fifteen years. The College's School of Education has created an array of opportunities in the form of student placements, research, adjunct instructor recruitment, student recruitment, and teacher professional development.

Manhattanville faculty teach some of their courses at Edison. Manhattanville teacher candidates get experience in the classrooms, beginning with observations and ending with a student teaching semester. The College's faculty use Edison's faculty and students as participants in their research. Edison faculty teach graduate education courses, both on site and often in conjunction with the after-school program and on Manhattanville's campus. Edison's students have a connection with the College, see college as a possibility, and are potential first-generation undergraduate students. Edison teachers enroll in Manhattanville's graduate programs for professional development and master's degrees.

POTENTIAL PARTNERS' OUTLOOK ON PARTNERSHIPS WITH SCHOOLS

Business, community organizations, and colleges/universities look to schools and their districts to promote their services and products and extend their reach. School-business partnerships promote free advertising, widen client bases, and broaden visibility about the quality of their product or service to the entire community. These partnerships create knowledgeable consumers and develop a future workforce.

Community organizations fulfill their missions, live their visions, reach their goals, and improve their organizations with school-community partnerships. Their work with children in schools puts them at the ground level in developing the next generation of citizens and community leaders. Colleges

Table 2.1 What's In It For Me? WIIFM?

Question	Response
What do I need? / What can I give?	
How do I get it? / How can I give it?	
When do I need it? / When can I give it?	
Where do I get it? / Where do I give it?	
How much time can I give? / How much time do I need?	
How much can I spend? / How much can I receive?	
Who are the key people?	
Does the partnership support the goals?	

and universities need relationships with schools to develop future college-ready students and conduct research. Schools of education need schools to place and prepare future teachers.

Partnerships with schools support the needs of all parties and stakeholders when the purposes are mutually beneficial. Consider all types of school partnerships. Complete the chart in table 2.1 to identify what would be a prospective partner's incentive to work with your school or school district. Look at the partnership from both your perspective and the prospective partner's point of view. Which type(s) of partnership(s) aligns with your needs? Matches your goals? Has capacity to partner? Think locally, nationally, and internationally. If the WIIFMs match, a partnership can develop.

Chapter 3

Guidelines for Entrepreneurial Leaders in Building Partnerships

After a yearlong search, the Board of Education hired Superintendent Barks to "save the district" from its fiscal mismanagement and ever-growing achievement gap. Once revered in the region as a district with an abundance of resources, top-notch students, and a supportive parent community, the district has dropped in ranking and suffered in reputation.

Superintendent Barks was appointed because of his previous success in a district with similar challenges. He worked with his district and community stakeholders to help them understand what had to be done with the budget, personnel, programs, and partnerships to change the district's trajectory. What is it about Superintendent Barks that has contributed to his success? What do his characteristics and actions have to do with building partnerships?

Superintendent Barks understood that he needed to help his new district redirect itself so that it would be accepting of its current student and community profile rather than dismissive of it. He also needed to help the district balance its budget. With "fresh eyes" he was able to analyze expenditures for personnel, instructional programs, facilities, and special initiatives, and identify areas in need of reduction and expansion. He knew that he must get buy-in from his stakeholders—administrators, teachers, staff, parents, community, partners—to put into place a plan that shifted the district's spending policies and patterns.

FIRST STEPS IN MOVING A DISTRICT FORWARD

Superintendent Barks began by communicating to his cabinet of district administrators his discoveries of spending practices within and across schools. He explained why the usual spending practices, even longstanding ones, had to cease. He enlisted their help in reviewing carefully all budgetary requests so that, together, they could determine the necessity of proposed expenditures. He established a system of review with his business administrator to facilitate decision-making. Although apologetic for the time-consuming nature of this task, he helped his cabinet understand that a collaborative and collective system of review provided a united message to the community about a new and different approach to fiscal management of the district.

As his cabinet members began to appreciate reasons for the district's downward spiral, they also started to communicate to their respective constituencies convincing data about decisions that had to be made to "save the district." Even though their teams of administrators and teachers were initially upset by the cabinet's refusal to honor longstanding items in the budget, they eventually understood that the district's mismanagement had to be rectified for the district's survival.

Superintendent Barks' analysis also revealed the insularity of the district in collaborating with businesses, the community, and universities to stimulate growth. He found that his previous district's partnerships added immeasurably to students' learning opportunities. He helped his cabinet understand the need to consider ways in which other entities might strengthen programs and provide desired resources at minimal or even no cost. Of immediate interest to Superintendent Barks was the elementary mathematics curriculum because of students' embarrassingly low scores on the statewide tests and the lack of a cohesive program across the district.

He demonstrated with various data tables ways in which the mathematics curriculum was hindering students' achievement. He explained that he had found a potential partner who would assist the district with both curricular cohesion and differentiated instruction for the students' varied academic and linguistic backgrounds. Instead of working directly with publishers, he wanted the district to work with a local educational consulting firm with expert mathematics educators who would assess students' needs and create an individualized mentoring program for teachers. This mentoring program would develop teachers' content knowledge and teaching strategies for students with diverse learning needs.

The firm would then work with the teachers and administrators to select an appropriate program for all elementary schools. The firm agreed to work with the district for two years. This firm understood that its profit would come from the publishing company ultimately selected, and not from the district. It was the firm's chance to promote itself by working with an important school district in the region to overhaul the curriculum. Superintendent Barks explained that he had learned about this firm at a regional conference and then investigated it thoroughly before bringing the idea forward.

As with the budget, and once his cabinet was supportive, Superintendent Barks used a variety of face-to-face and virtual forums to communicate frequently to his stakeholders about how this partnership would strengthen the district's mathematics curriculum.

THINKING AND ACTING ENTREPRENEURIALLY

According to Christoph Winkler, Endowed Professor and Founding Director of the Hynes Institute for Entrepreneurship & Innovation at Iona College in New Rochelle, New York, Superintendent Barks represents an entrepreneurial leader. He took ownership of his ideas, acted on his ideas, communicated his ideas to the appropriate stakeholders, received buy-in, and worked with his constituency to achieve what became common goals for the district's financial and academic well-being.

Christoph, who is also a well-regarded scholar and thought-leader in entrepreneurship education, believes that entrepreneurial leadership can be developed in K-12 school leaders. Such leaders need to navigate differently but can do so by observing what others are doing in different contexts, bringing ideas back to their own context, and helping others within their communities to reenvision new possibilities for their schools.

In order to be successful, these leaders need to self-reflect on and learn from their incremental successes and failures (Guiding questions: Did I achieve my incremental goals? Why or why not?) as they pursue their desired outcomes. This process requires a continuous adaptation of their incremental goals and strategies based on the learning that took place (Personal Communication, September 4, 2018).

Entrepreneurial educational leaders understand how to establish priorities for their districts and how to strategically leverage resources and pursue opportunities with discipline and passion. They do not necessarily wait for others to reach out. Rather, they make overtures to others to explore options.

They understand that they need stakeholder buy-in, but also are comfortable with the messiness of trial and error. They want to empower their stakeholders, especially their teachers, and know that they must help them to tolerate disruption for the sake of creating new opportunities for teaching and learning (Hess & McShane, 2016). They acknowledge that they and their stakeholders must break away from traditional operating methods (Davis & Molnar, 2014).

Even with the challenges of working in a traditionally bureaucratic and mission-driven structure, entrepreneurial education leaders figure out ways to empower, motivate, and communicate with their teachers so that they want to participate (Lynch, 2016b). They use their interpersonal skills to help their teachers and other stakeholders see the benefits of new pursuits.

Such leaders believe in Carol Dweck's growth mentality because they are coachable, willing to take risks, change direction as necessary, and face their own strengths and limitations (Kurshan, 2017). They understand that partnerships present both promises and challenges because of the imprecise arrangements that solidify over time, yet are excited to forge ahead.

GATHERING DATA TO CREATE ELEVATOR SPEECHES FOR POTENTIAL PARTNERSHIPS

Entrepreneurial educational leaders understand the value of quid pro quo. To get something from a potential partner they must be able to offer something in return. Such leaders need to know enough about their schools and districts to know what is needed from partners. They must engage in a comprehensive assessment before moving forward with partnership initiatives. This investigative work ultimately saves time and energy and provides the foundation for an *elevator speech* that eventually is needed to convince potential partners about an institution's value.

An elevator speech is a quick synopsis that describes a process, product, service, or organization and its value potential. It is called an elevator speech because it takes the time to ride an elevator from the ground floor to the exit floor. It usually lasts for thirty to sixty seconds but could be as long as two minutes.

Elevator speeches should include an overview and unique aspects of the school or district, reasons for the partnership, and ways in which the partnership would be mutually beneficial. Effective elevator speeches engage the listener, convince the listener of the fit between the two institutions, and entice the listener to want to learn more (Gregory, 2018; Sherman, 2017). School and district leaders use the data gathered about their organizations, stakeholders, and programs to include in their elevator speeches.

Examples of Elevator Speeches

The two examples—one from a superintendent and one from a principal—include basic information about the students, teachers, parents, community, and curriculum. The content of elevator speeches can provide the springboard for comprehensive partnership proposals.

Business-Middle School Partnership. A group of superintendents learned that a technology corporation located in the region was going to donate 100 laptops to a school district. In exchange, a school district would need to demonstrate student growth in relation to the district's learning goals. This corporation's motivation for this business-school partnership was to help schools better prepare students for STEM (Science, Technology, Engineering, and Mathematics) careers. One superintendent, intent on getting this donation for her district, prepared the following elevator speech for the director of the partnership grant.

Argos School District believes in addressing its achievement gap though inclusion. Students from all neighborhoods attend each of the four elementary schools, the middle school, and the high school. The racial composition of the district is 38 percent Black, 35 percent Hispanic, 20 percent White, and 7 percent Asian. There is a wide range with students' standardized test scores that reflect students' socioeconomic status and racial background. Hispanic parents are at a disadvantage because many do not speak English. The teachers are mostly white, middle-class, mid-career, and highly educated.

The Argos community believes in the schools. Merchants and community groups provide whatever support they can. Community support helps to fulfill the mission of educating the whole child. Multiple services—medical, dental, psychological, counseling—are provided because professionals donate their time. Argos also has a strong science program because of support from the local pharmaceutical companies.

Our next focus, as we strengthen STEM education, is on technology. We need teachers to use technology on a regular basis so that students capitalize on technology's benefits for problem-solving. If we were to receive your grant of 100 laptops, we would put them in the sixth grade in the middle school. The math and science teachers, who work in teams, are poised to work with the district technology coordinator to revise the math and science curriculum to integrate technology. Our district's research coordinator will set up an assessment system to measure students' growth because of technology use.

If you form the partnership with our district, you will be working with a highly diverse district that has talented teachers who will follow through with whatever plan we put into place. We are focused on STEM, have a very supportive Board of Education that will be very proud to publicize this partnership, and we believe that we can show the growth you are looking for in STEM subjects, particularly for our less fortunate students.

University-Primary School Partnership. A principal of a K-1 school is trying to get help for his teachers. He does not want to have to hire teacher assistants because they are not affordable or do not have the educational background that he is seeking. He learned from a colleague that he should appeal to the local university to get graduate students seeking master's degrees in early childhood. He used the following elevator speech to appeal to the university's education dean.

We are interested in bringing your early childhood students to Kepher Elementary School. Our K-1 school houses all the children in the district who are primarily from blue collar or impoverished backgrounds. Eighty percent of our children are Black or Hispanic. The parents, most of whom are hardworking, have difficulty attending school events. The teachers, all with master's degrees in early childhood education, are so dedicated that they visit their students' homes or attend community events to try to engage parents as much as possible.

Our early childhood curriculum has been cited as a model program because of our combined focus on both skill development and play. We have spent many years developing the curriculum to address the varying needs of our diverse student population. We want to ensure that our students begin second grade prepared and motivated.

If your university would commit to sending your early childhood majors to our school, we would work with you and your faculty to offer coursework to your students at our school site and will pay your students $10,000 a year to work alongside Kepher teachers as their assistants. Your students would need to make a commitment to work at Kepher for two years. However, they would be able to do their student teaching during the second year.

When your students graduate, they will have had two full years in the field and will receive a stipend for their fieldwork. If teaching positions in Kepher become available, we promise to consider them first for employment. Our expert teachers are excited to work with your students, and our early childhood coordinator will oversee the entire program. Your students will be exposed to a diverse student population, expert teachers, a model early childhood curriculum, a commitment from us to hire them if jobs become available, and unique approaches to parent outreach.

MAJOR AREAS FOR DATA COLLECTION FOR POSSIBLE PARTNERSHIPS

Data are powerful indicators about your school or district's academic and organizational focus. Data about students, teachers, parents, community, curriculum, and resources become part of the story that you tell about your institution's unique identity and contribute to convincing others about needs and challenges (Davis & Molnar, 2014). These data will entice potential partners.

Students

Who are your students?

- Nationalities?
- Ethnicities?
- Religions?
- Linguistic backgrounds?
- Socioeconomic status?
- Achievement and learning profiles?
- Special learning needs?
- Behavioral challenges?
- Home life?
- Neighborhood activities?

New school leaders especially need to learn as much as possible about their student population. In addition to ensuring that data are available at the school and district levels, it is useful to tap into the following:

- teachers' anecdotal knowledge of students' learning strengths and weaknesses across content areas
- behavioral and social tendencies in the classroom and social spaces such as the playground and lunchroom
- key features about their family situations (Wepner, Gómez, Cunningham, Rainville, & Kelly, 2016).

Teachers can assess students' linguistic proclivities in relation to their backgrounds and can provide profiles of their students in relation to district standards. Focus groups with teachers, meetings with administrative staff, classroom visitations, attendance at parent events, meetings with community leaders, and informal drop-ins at community events contribute to a comprehensive profile of the students in your schools. These outreach efforts provide invaluable information about students' learning achievements and needs. See chapters 4, 5, and 6 for additional information on how partnerships can affect students.

Teachers

Information about teachers should focus on their demographic profiles and their special qualities. Demographic information should include their age, sex, racial/ethnic/cultural/religious background, years of teaching experience, and level of degree completion. Information about their special qualities should include their level of success and extracurricular activities with students, professional development pursuits, community involvement, unique skills and traits, and reputation.

This information highlights the teaching staff, identifies professional development needs, and captures instructional capabilities within and across grades and content areas. The identification of teachers' professional development needs will prompt schools and districts to determine what they can provide internally and what they need to seek externally.

Elementary principal Kathy Rifka discovered that her fourth and fifth teachers did not know how to properly use the reading assessment that the district had adopted for all the K-5 schools. She did not have a reading background, did not have a reading specialist in the building, and could not rely on the district English Language Arts coordinator to mentor her teachers. She also did not have the funds to hire a consultant to work with her teachers for an extended period of time.

She knew that the literacy department at the local university had an excellent reputation because she herself had been serving as an adjunct instructor at the college in the educational leadership program. She reached out to the department chair of the literacy department to see whether the faculty would be interested in forming a partnership that would enable their students to do their practicum at her school if one or more of their faculty would work with her teachers to learn how to administer the assessment system. Within a month, they had a partnership agreement signed.

Two literacy professors agreed to mentor her teachers. Each professor took a grade level. They worked with them individually and by grade level. They reintroduced the assessment system, modeled its administration, and helped the teachers to analyze student data in relation to instructional decision-making. They then worked with the teachers in their individual classrooms to model and support them during the next round of assessments to make sure they knew what to do. These two professors used the fourth and fifth grade classrooms as site-based classrooms for their master's degree students.

Parents

Given that parental influence on children's success in school is undeniable, it is critical to find out who the parents are, what their needs are, and how best the school and district can respond. A demographic profile or composite description of the parent community that exists in each school building helps to understand parents' employment, academic, socioeconomic, linguistic, and ethnic/cultural/religious characteristics. Parents' perceptions about how the schools are helping and can help their children are equally important. Surveys or home visits can be used (Edwards, Domke, & White, 2017).

If families speak a language other than English, surveys and home visits need to be in parents' native language. Parents' responses to questions about what they believe that the schools are doing, or not doing, to help their children helps to establish a list of priorities for addressing unmet needs and requests. These priorities can serve as a basis for additional communication and outreach opportunities.

A school or district can enlist professional coaches and athletes, local political leaders, the Boys and Girls Club, the United Way, recreation centers, and the library (Milner, 2015). Schools also can recruit and train willing community members such as social workers, coaches, and high school National Honor Society members to serve as mentors and role models for parents (Edwards, Domke, & White, 2017). These outreach initiatives can lead to partnership prospects with your community.

Community

Each community, which refers to all those within and outside of the school walls, has its own history and resources. School leaders need to cultivate relationships with their communities so that they can learn as much as possible about what is available for their students and their families. Connections with the community can be made through face-to-face conversations, visitations to events (as mentioned above in trying to learn about students), and social media interaction. Efforts to learn about and interact with the community help to appreciate what life is like for students and their families.

Teams of teachers, administrators, and students, or any combination, can participate in collaborative research projects to find out information about the following:

- Organizations that exist in the community (churches, businesses, etc.)
- Geography and architecture of the community (flat, renewal, rural, etc.)
- Types of housing available (single-family, apartment, etc.)
- Different kinds of employment (government, industry, construction, etc.)
- Issues that you observe (trash, graffiti, potholes, parks, etc.) and location
- Evidence of construction/reconstruction/renovation/repair (O'Sullivan, 2001; Remillard, 2001; Wepner et al., 2016).

This information can be quite useful when creating a district/community profile for partnerships beyond the region. For partnerships within the region, the local Chamber of Commerce can help to identify the businesses that exist within the community that want to partner with schools (Sloan, 2008).

Curriculum

In reviewing your school or district's curriculum, engage in big picture thinking about the content and skills that you want your students to have and the instructional practices that your teachers are using. You want your curriculum and teachers' pedagogy to be culturally responsive and relevant to your students. You want to assess any gaps or overlaps within the curriculum.

The Understanding by Design (UbD) framework, which is based upon the concept of backward design, helps to guide the development of curriculum by beginning with the end in mind (McTighe & Wiggins, 2005). Efforts to engage in curriculum mapping begin by thinking about the desired outcomes and then considering enduring understandings and essential questions that guide instruction for students. The question that is asked is "What should students know, understand, and be able to do?" In answering this question, goals are set for students that then hone in on desirable instructional methodologies and resources (Wepner et al., 2016).

Any gaps that are identified between goals and deliverables can serve as the impetus for reaching out to potential partners to help students achieve critical learning goals.

Resources

While resources come primarily from the district's budget to assist with students, teachers, parents, community outreach, and the curriculum, partnerships can provide personnel, goods, and services to help supplement the budget. Partnerships can provide mentors and tutors, unique experiential learning opportunities, professional development, health services for parents, and even new physical facilities.

Sue Ostrofsky, formerly principal of Mount Kisco Elementary School in Bedford, New York, figured out how to build partnerships to get additional resources to support her schools.

An article written in a local newspaper a few years back reported that it only takes half a second to realize that Sue Ostrofsky, now principal of Fox Lane Middle School in Bedford Central School District, New York, loves her job. She has been characterized as having the energy of a tornado as she moves through each day on behalf of her students, faculty, administrative staff, and parents.

Her talents are so valued by her community that the school district determined that after serving as the principal of the most diverse elementary school in the district for twelve years, she was needed in the district's one middle school to help bring together a divided community of haves and have-nots.

Sue watched her elementary school grow more diverse and double in size from under 300 students to nearly 600 students while she was principal. She used her proactive, entrepreneurial behavior and optimistic outlook to organize her teaching staff to achieve a common goal of helping her diverse student body succeed more robustly with both informal and formal assessments.

She worked with her staff to develop programs and acquire resources that would help with achievement.

Many of these resources came from her partnership initiatives. She knew that she needed additional assistance in the classrooms and professional development for her teachers as she implemented a dual language program and embarked on an assessment of the reading program in the early grades. She formed a Professional Development School with Manhattanville College so that she could hire its graduate teacher candidates as interns and its faculty as professional development consultants.

Through the partnership, she brought college professors in to provide support to her faculty in these endeavors. She encouraged her teachers to participate and present at the annual Changing Suburbs Institute® Education Forum. Sue networked at the college's events in search of even more resources for her school (more information about the formation of a Professional Development School is in chapter 6).

Graduate education students became paid interns who helped the teachers in the classrooms, and also worked as substitute teachers when needed. The district had created a program to hire graduate education students to serve as substitute teachers for approximately 100 days and pre-student teaching interns for 80 days. The interns could opt to student teach (unpaid) in the district during the second year of the program and continue with the paid internship afterwards.

Sue enlisted the college faculty to help her teachers learn about culturally relevant pedagogy, especially with literacy instruction. As a strong believer in preparing new teachers for the diverse classrooms of the twenty-first century, Sue served as a panelist at the college symposium that was focused on characteristics of successful new teachers.

Now at the middle school, Sue is using her same entrepreneurial leadership skills to organize and motivate her staff to achieve common objectives through innovation and take advantage of internal and external opportunities. Since her middle school also is a Professional Development School (PDS) with Manhattanville College, she has been using funds set aside for this PDS to enable teams of teachers to develop cross-curricular units. She is working with her college liaison to reenergize the internship program so that she can attract teacher candidates who want to teach at the middle-school level.

College faculty also are coming to her school to serve as consultants for curriculum development work and co-teachers in specific disciplines. To help her diverse student population, most of which come from her elementary school, she turns to her college liaison to organize a visitation to the college so that they learn firsthand about the benefits of college. She uses funds set aside for the PDS to pay for bus transportation. Sue understands that the formal partnerships that she has formed, whether with the college or other *organizations, have enabled her to bring opportunities to her school that ordinarily would not be available.*

BEGIN YOUR PLAN FOR DEVELOPING PARTNERSHIPS

There is no surefire way to develop partnerships. Some find partnership opportunities by happenstance through a networking event of colleague leaders; some receive cold calls from potential partners who are looking to connect with schools; and some follow a methodical course of action, with intense fact-finding missions, that lead to intriguing prospects. The following guidelines are general strategies that leaders have used to develop partnerships. These guidelines require a combination of independent research, collaborative work with stakeholders, community outreach, and persuasive communication.

Work with a Group of Like-Minded Individuals

Identify your group of individuals who can recognize and articulate needs, consider opportunities' pros and cons, go willingly on fact-finding missions, develop rational proposals, energize others, and create realistic partnership possibilities for your school or district. It could be an existing cabinet of administrators, a standing leadership team of teachers and/or administrators, or a newly formed committee of representative stakeholders from the district that extend to parents, community members, and students.

This group needs to be willing to meet as often as needed, work in between meetings, be forward thinking about forming partnerships, take risks on behalf of the school and district, and be open to the idea of reaching beyond existing structures. You need individuals who are big picture and detail oriented, and thinkers and doers (South Washington County School District, n.d.). Once you have a team in place, identify a chair or co-chairs who are responsible for bringing the group together on a regular basis, and with a purposeful agenda for each meeting. This group needs to:

- Understand the school or district's needs and challenges with students, teachers, parents, community, curriculum, and resources. Compare the needs and challenges identified with any type of school improvement plan. Condense the two documents into a list of five major goals that should be addressed.
- Gather information about any previous partnerships. Identify the types of partnerships that existed and the outcomes for each. Specify strengths and weaknesses of these partnerships, including those responsible at each institution. Determine reasons for success and failure.

- Establish goals and objectives for new partnerships. Use fact-finding efforts about the school's or district's needs and previous partnership activities to determine ways in which new partnerships can help with the district's five major goals.
- Identify the types of partners needed. Use information from chapter 2 to decide on the types of partners to pursue. Such decisions will be based on partners that could be available, connections with possible partners, previous partnership successes, and overtures from potential partners. Connections with possible partners could include children of business employees or school employees who are spouses, relatives, or friends.

Table 3.1 provides a sample chart for a potential business partnership that identifies school needs, possible business needs, and partnership possibilities that can address the needs of both entities. Use this type of chart as a first step in determining how partnerships will support school needs. Table 3.2 includes a sample service and resource form to help assess the potential for community partnerships. Use this type of form to better understand ways in which different types of businesses, community organizations, and universities can provide needed services.

Find and Communicate with Potential Partners

After working with your team to identify potential partners, find individuals to contact. Figure out the best way to communicate. You can write, call, or stop by the partner's location. Visits are the most effective. This gives you the opportunity to give your elevator speech. If that is not possible, phone calls are more effective than letters (South Washington County School District, n.d.). Again, your elevator speech can be put to good use. If you do not already have an elevator speech or written proposal, prepare an outline of your ideas for the partnership to use as a springboard for your conversation.

Table 3.1 Sample Chart for Matching School Needs with Business Resources

School Needs	Business Needs	Partnership Possibilities
Safe place for after-school activities	Lower employee absenteeism	After-school center for school-aged children, possibly staffed by teachers
Increasing student passing scores	Increased volunteerism	Business employees serve as tutors
Money management curriculum	Skilled workforce	Business employees work with teachers and administrators to develop curriculum. Business employees given time to teach program Adolescents intern at business site

Table 3.2 Service and Resource Form to Assess Potential for Community Partnership

Name of Community Organization: _____

Contact Person: _____

Community Organization's Mission and Goals:

Capacity of Community Organization Services:	Available Resources for K-12 Schools and Families:
Current Community Outreach Initiatives:	Types of Previous and Current Projects:

Larger organizations probably require a good deal of detail in the outline or proposal (Finkel, 2013).

ESTABLISH PARTNERSHIPS

Once communication with a viable partner leads you to believe that you are ready to take the next steps, schedule one or more meetings that bring together members of both institutions to formulate collaborative plans. The meeting(s) can be face-to-face, virtual, or by telephone. Create an agenda that includes the following topics:

- Brief overview of each institution
- Reason for the proposed partnership
- Proposed goals, outcomes, and activities
- Roles and responsibilities of each partner
- Management structure
- Internal and external communication plans and expectations
- Launch date and plans to kick off the partnership.

There should be an atmosphere of positive thinking and mutual respect at these meetings so that each institution's representatives leave with a feeling of excitement for partnering together. Before or after your meetings, make sure that you have visited the partnership site, and vice versa, if relevant to the partnership.

Identify Key Person(s) Responsible

Identify one or more persons responsible for the many facets of partnership development and sustainability. It could be you. It could be different people for different partnerships. Justin Aglio, Director of Academic Achievement and District Innovation at Montour School District in McKees Rocks, Pennsylvania (see chapter 4 for his vignette) explained that he often initiates partnerships and then has a team of administrators and teachers who are directly involved with different partnerships at different times.

Superintendent Barks from the opening vignette determined that it is best to have his principals responsible for working directly with the educational consulting firm that will help with the district's elementary mathematics curriculum. His principals can ensure that the firm's interactions with the students and teachers are in line with their school's culture.

Superintendent Barks also appreciates that his principals know firsthand the type of activities that can be supported in a school, the teachers and staff who will support the partnership, the kinds of release time needed for teachers and staff to participate in selecting a new mathematics curriculum, and ways in which to sustain participation. He also has designated a central office administrator to oversee the coordination of the consulting firm's work, the selection of the curriculum, and the execution of all partnership paperwork.

Those responsible need to be wholeheartedly supportive of partnership opportunities, aware of the promises and challenges of the partnership in relation to the context in which the partnership will be implemented, and skilled at creating parameters and conditions for the partnership to thrive.

Seek Approval

The type of official approval needed depends on your position within the school district and the complexity of the partnership. Approval should be sought vertically (hierarchically) and horizontally. Superintendents may need Board approval. Central office administrators need superintendents' approval. Principals typically need central office administrators' approval and so forth.

Additionally, administrators at any of these levels should seek nods of approval from their teachers and administrative staff. They might also want the tacit approval from the parents and community, depending on the type of partnership. Parent and community approval would be important for partnerships that require structural changes to buildings, alternative programs, significant funding changes, or the addition of districtwide instructional options.

Execute Written Agreements

Written agreements clarify and record expectations and terms associated with the partnership. They are invaluable if there is turnover in partners and/or disagreements during project implementation. They also are useful in orienting individuals who are new to an established partnership. Usually called a Memorandum of Understanding (MOU), a written agreement includes information about the purpose of the agreement, partnership roles and responsibilities, terms of agreement and payment structure, legal protections for each partner, and the expectations and conditions for data collection during the partnership.

- Purpose of the agreement. What is the purpose of the partnership? In what ways will the goals be implemented?
- Partnership roles and responsibilities. Who is the agreement between? What are the roles and responsibilities of each partner? Who will be the signatories on the agreement?
- Project direction. What are the goals of the partnership? In what ways will the goals be implemented?
- Terms of agreement and payment structure. When is the start date and end date of the partnership? What type of payment is involved? How will such payments be carried out?
- Legal protections for each partner. What protections are there for each stakeholder? What nondiscrimination policies need to be followed? What conditions are in place for each partner to be able to terminate the agreement? What is the status of each contractor?
- Data collection. If data are collected, will either/both partners be able to disseminate/publish findings? What type of data can be collected? (Collaborative Center for Health Equity, n.d.).

MOUs will vary, depending on the nature and complexity of the partnership and institutional expectations for establishing agreements. Some agreements include basic, general information, while others detail every possible facet of the partnership. Agreements can be brief one-pagers or multiple pages of narrative texts. It is important to have a lawyer or MOU expert review agreements before they are signed.

Figures 3.1 and 3.2 provide examples of partnership agreements that have been adapted from two different school districts that could be used for business, community, or university partnerships (Henrico Schools Partnership

| School partner (Print) | Business/University/Community partner (Print) |

Partner Address:

Partner is: o Business o University o Community group

Nature of partnership (Check as many as applicable):

o Staff support
o Administrative/clerical support
o Direct assistance to students
o Contribution of materials, equipment, or funds. Monetary value of contribution: $_____
o Other: _____

If applicable, give estimate of projected hours of volunteer time per week, month or year. *(Example: Two people each volunteering four hours per month – eight volunteer hours per month):* _____ hours per _____.

Note: Each in-school volunteer must complete a volunteer application and present it at the school. The form and guidelines can be found at [URL].

Purpose of partnership:

State specific expectations for both partners; this should include roles and responsibilities of each.

The school will:

The partner will:

It is understood by both parties that this partnership will remain in place for the current school year and will continue under the same terms until terminated by either partner or modified by both parties. The School Board reserves the right to terminate the agreement without penalty at any time if it determines that the agreement is having an adverse impact on the educational experience of students.

| School representative (Signature) | Date | (Print name) |

| Partner representative (Signature) | Date | (Print name) |

Figure 3.1 School Partnership Agreement Form. *Source*: Adapted from Henrico County School District (2016, August). Henrico schools partnership agreement form. Retrieved from http://henricoschools.us/pdf/Community/PartnershipAgreement.pdf.

Chapter 3

| SCHOOL NAME | AND | PARTNER NAME |

This agreement is completed by the school principal and partner liaison. Both parties should maintain a file copy.

School Name		Partner Name	
School Leader/Title		Partner Leader/Title	
Mailing Address/Zip		Mailing Address/Zip	
Phone	Email	Phone	Email
Primary Contact/Coordinator Name		Primary Contact/Coordinator Name	

Partnership Start Date: _____ End Date: _____ Annual Review Date: _____

Partnership Resource Contributions
# of Volunteers, Mentors and/or Speakers: _____
Estimated # of Hours: _____
Estimated Financial/Product donation: $_____
Shared Partner Goal(s):

School Contributions
Estimated Materials Costs: _____
Advertising/Promotions: _____

Partner Goals(s):
Partner Commitments:
School Goal(s):
School Commitments:

Criminal background screenings are required for all volunteers. The principal has the decision-making authority regarding volunteers and volunteer opportunities in the schools.

Signatures

_____

School Partner—Printed Principal Name and Signature   Date

_____

Partner—Printed Name and Signature   Date

Figure 3.2 School/Business/Community/University Partner Agreement. *Source*: Adapted from South Washington County School District. (n.d.). Toolkit for building partnerships between schools and business or organization South Washington County Schools. Retrieved from https://docplayer.net/5550265-Toolkit-for-building-partnerships-between-schools-and-businesses-or-organizations-across-south-washington-county-schools.html.

Agreement Form, 2016; South Washington County School District, n.d.). Textbox 3.1 provides a sample MOU between a school district and a university to form a Professional Development School.

TEXTBOX 3.1   SAMPLE PROFESSIONAL DEVELOPMENT PARTNERSHIP AGREEMENT

This agreement, which goes into effect on (DATE), is between (NAME OF SCHOOL) Professional Development School (PDS), (NAME OF SCHOOL DISTRICT) and (NAME OF UNIVERSITY). These organizations have formed a partnership to strengthen their professional and program development initiatives for practicing and prospective teachers and the school community. The following establishes the agreements and services that will be provided by the (NAME OF UNIVERSITY), as the contractor, and (NAME OF SCHOOL AND DISTRICT), the service recipient.

1. Responsibilities of (NAME OF UNIVERSITY):

(NAME OF UNIVERSITY) is responsible for:

a) Providing a Professional Development School (PDS) liaison to the school. This PDS liaison, a full-time or part-time faculty member, will work at the school for a total of two days each week. This PDS liaison will oversee all PDS initiatives, and help to bring programs and resources to the school for the professional development of teachers. This PDS liaison also supervises student teachers
b) Committing funds for the PDS Liaison
c) Assuming any expenses in advertising and searching for the appropriate PDS liaison
d) Working collaboratively with the Principal of the PDS to hire the PDS liaison in compliance with (NAME OF UNIVERSITY)'s hiring processes
e) Establishing a separate budget item for the school district's annual contribution that is monitored by the PDS Principal, the PDS liaison, and the Dean of (NAME OF UNIVERSITY)
f) Working with (NAME OF SCHOOL DISTRICT) to continue to develop an evaluation protocol for the PDS
g) Providing teacher candidates for field experiences and student teaching as available
h) Providing on-site courses to the PDS as appropriate

i) Inviting qualified PDS teachers and administrators to serve as adjunct faculty, when appropriate and in compliance with (NAME OF UNIVERSITY)'s hiring processes
j) Writing grants with (NAME OF SCHOOL DISTRICT) to seek funding for special projects and initiatives
k) Offering a one-third tuition discount to all presently employed (NAME OF SCHOOL DISTRICT) faculty, administrative staff, and parents of sponsored dependents who currently are enrolled in (NAME OF SCHOOL DISTRICT) for undergraduate and graduate education courses
l) Providing discounted registration to (NAME OF UNIVERSITY) conferences to all (NAME OF SCHOOL DISTRICT) faculty and administrators
m) Providing a 50 percent discount of tuition at (NAME OF UNIVERSITY) of (NAME OF SCHOOL DISTRICT) who are accepted to attend (NAME OF UNIVERSITY) following graduation from high school. This discount will be renewable annually as long as the eligible student maintains satisfactory academic progress at (NAME OF UNIVERSITY)

2. **Responsibilities of** (NAME OF SCHOOL DISTRICT)

(NAME OF SCHOOL DISTRICT) is responsible for:

a) Contributing $ (AGREED PAYMENT STRUCTURE) to (NAME OF UNIVERSITY) for the year to support all PDS initiatives related to the professional development of teachers and program development for the school community. This contribution will help with special programming events and projects
b) Entrusting the Principal and the PDS liaison to create an annual budget for the expenditure of funds in collaboration with the PDS Steering Committee, with approval of the Dean of (NAME OF UNIVERSITY), to support the growth and development of the PDS
c) Committing to (NAME OF UNIVERSITY) so that (NAME OF SCHOOL) only has (NAME OF UNIVERSITY) teacher candidates for field experiences and student teaching
d) Working with (NAME OF UNIVERSITY) to identify criteria for hiring a PDS liaison and interviewing PDS liaison applicants in compliance with (NAME OF UNIVERSITY)'s hiring processes
e) Collaborating with the PDS liaison to develop mutually agreed upon programs
f) Continuing to develop an evaluation protocol for the PDS with (NAME OF UNIVERSITY)
g) Providing placements for field experiences and student teaching

h) Making all necessary arrangements to have (NAME OF SCHOOL) students visit (NAME OF UNIVERSITY)
i) Arranging to have (NAME OF UNIVERSITY) education courses offered on-site as appropriate
j) Working with the (NAME OF UNIVERSITY) to identify qualified teachers and administrators who can serve as adjunct faculty, when appropriate and in compliance with (NAME OF UNIVERSITY) hiring processes
k) Writing grants with the (NAME OF UNIVERSITY) to seek funding for special projects and initiatives
l) Providing space for the PDS liaison
m) Offering pre-student teaching (NAME OF UNIVERSITY) students reasonable access to (NAME OF SCHOOL) classrooms for the purpose of acquiring field observation hours
n) Providing (NAME OF UNIVERSITY) with adequate space one (1) day a week following the school day for the purpose of conducting student teaching seminar. This seminar shall be taught by a (NAME OF UNIVERSITY) field supervisor

3. Term of Agreement
MM/DD/Year through MM/DD/Year

4. Compliance with FERPA
(NAME OF SCHOOL DISTRICT) acknowledges that certain information about the college's students is contained in records maintained by the (NAME OF SCHOOL DISTRICT) and that this information can be confidential by reason of the Family and Educational Rights and Privacy Act of 1974 (20 U.S. C. 1232g) and related institution policies unless valid consent is obtained from the college's students or their legal guardians. Both parties agree to protect these records in accordance with FERPA and College policy. To the extent permitted by law, nothing contained herein shall be construed as precluding either party from releasing such information to the other so that each can perform its respective responsibilities.

5. Nondiscrimination
Both parties to this Agreement shall comply with all applicable federal, state, and local laws or regulations and the College's Nondiscrimination and Harassment Policy, in that no person shall, on the grounds of race, color, creed, religion, sexual orientation, national origin, age, sex, marital status, blindness, source of payment or sponsorship or disability, be

excluded from participation, be denied benefits of, or otherwise be subject to discrimination under any program, service, employment relationship, or activity offered by either party.

6. Method of Payment

The Professional Development School District will send a check to (NAME OF UNIVERSITY) on or about (DATE) to be put into a separate budget item designated for the PDS.

7. Termination of Agreement

Each member of this partnership reserves the right to cancel this agreement at any time should it determine that the need for services no longer exists.

8. Status of Contractor

It is understood and agreed by both parties that (NAME OF UNIVERSITY) is an independent contractor and not an employee of the (NAME OF UNIVERSITY) and that (NAME OF UNIVERSITY) is not entitled to any of the benefits or privileges accruing to employees of that organization. This agreement may not be amended except in writing signed by the parties.

7. Jurisdiction

This Agreement shall be governed by the laws of the State of (NAME OF STATE). If any portion of this Agreement is found by a court of competent jurisdiction to be invalid or unenforceable, the remainder of this Agreement shall remain in full force and effect.

(NAME OF SUPERINTENDENT)
Superintendent

Date

(NAME OF PRINCIPAL)
Principal

Date

(NAME OF UNIVERSITY PRESIDENT)
President

Date

(NAME OF DEAN OF SCHOOL)
Dean
School of Education

Date

Adjust Arrangements to Accommodate Multiple Partnerships

Although the information above focuses on one partnership at a time, it is possible that you are engaged in a three-way or even four-way partnership opportunity. For example, you might want to form a partnership with a local oil company and a local university to promote an innovative STEAM (Science Technology Engineering Arts Mathematics) curriculum. The oil company would provide the equipment and the university would provide the faculty and students to help the teachers implement the curriculum.

Rather than two-way conversations, meetings, and agreements, there would be three-way discussions and documents that articulate shared goals and outcomes. While a bit more complicated, especially with attorneys' reviews, multi-institutional partnerships offer exciting growth opportunities when multiple perspectives are valued and incorporated into plans and activities.

CREATE A BLUEPRINT FOR IMPLEMENTATION AND EVALUATION

Provide and Ensure Preparation and Training for Partnership

If it is show time(!) for a partnership, it means that those in front of and behind the audience (or stakeholders) have had to prepare for the big event or launch. The launch could be the opening of a special room in the high school dedicated to biotechnology or in the middle school dedicated to music education. It could be the implementation of a new curriculum centered on creating a sustainable future or global education. It could be a special literacy project that brings literacy tutors to each primary classroom to work with children before, during, and after school.

Any of these launches need preparation and training of individuals who will be directly involved with the partnership activities. The type and intensity of the training depends on the planned partnership activities. For example, if volunteer tutors are coming into the building to work with children, they need to know about protocols for access to the building at different times of the day, teachers' expectations with instructional strategies, materials, and student interaction. The teachers need to be prepared to receive the tutors so that they can assign students, determine the tutors' tasks, and prepare their classrooms and students for this shift.

As the school or district leader, you want to ensure that both your partners and your own staff are prepared enough to feel confident that they are ready to launch the partnership. Preparation can include a brief or daylong orientation, a series of workshops or seminars, or one-on-one or small-group mentoring.

Such preparation could be conducted by a school-based person, a representative from the partnership, a third-party consultant, or any combination. You also want to assure that those peripherally involved are aware of the partnership's purpose so that there is overall support for the launch.

Prepare Teachers, Students, and Parents for Partnership. Safeguard against any backlash by assisting teachers, students, and parents in understanding the impact of the partnership on their day-to-day functioning, both short-term and long-term. Help teachers and parents appreciate the benefit of the partnership, even if they are not directly involved from the outset.

Explain what is expected to happen with the students, if relevant, within the school(s), and across the district. Discuss how it fits with the school district's mission, especially in relation to anticipated outcomes. Provide opportunities for questions and the expression of concerns. Communicate how you will address concerns. Introduce your key personnel responsible for partnership oversight so that they have access to persons who can address their issues on a regular basis.

Communicate with the Community

The scope and complexity of the partnership will determine the extent of communication with and involvement of the community. Some partnerships might require budget approval whereas others simply necessitate information sharing. If important for the success of the partnership, community members at large should have a place on an oversight board. They should have access to current information through the media, the district's website, and letters from you about partnership highlights.

Such information should include photographs of partners and students in the name of the partnership working together. Create a system and let them know about the system for receiving feedback from community members so that they know that their voices will be heard.

Develop System for Assessing Outcomes

A system for assessing outcomes ensures that the partnership is functioning the way it is intended to operate. Your assessment of the partnership's impact for short-term agreements can include face-to-face, email, or telephone conversations with participants to inquire about the success of activities. Your assessments for recurring or long-term agreements might also include surveys, multiple activity assessments, and annual evaluations. Figure 3.3 provides an example of an activity assessment, and Figure 3.4 provides an example of an annual evaluation that can be used to determine

School: _____   School Year: _____

Partner: _____

School Coordinator:	Partner Coordinator:
Phone:	Phone:
Email:	Email:

Activity Information

Name /Type of activity: _____ Date of activity: _____

Specific target groups involved: _____

Number of people involved in target groups: _____

Volunteers Used (hours) _____ Monetary Resources Used ($ amount) _____

Other Resources Used (please list):
What worked well?
What needs to change to make the activity more successful in the future?

Is there need for additional participants? _____ How many? _____
Who needs to be involved? _____

Figure 3.3 Annual Partnership Evaluation Form. *Source*: South Washington County School District. (n.d.). Toolkit for building partnerships between schools and business or organization South Washington County Schools. Retrieved from https://docplayer.net/555 0265-Toolkit-for-building-partnerships-between-schools-and-businesses-or-organization s-across-south-washington-county-schools.html.

Partnership Information

School: _____ School Year: _____

Partner: _____

School Coordinator:	Partner Coordinator:
Phone:	Phone:
Email:	Email:

Activity Summary Statistics

Total number of activities:	
Total number of school employees involved:	Total number of partner employees involved:
Total number of students involved:	Total number of volunteers involved:
Resources: School/Partner Total	
Total Volunteer Hours spent on activities	
Other in-kind resources (please list):	

Total monetary resources spent on or contributed toward activities $ _____

Overall Assessment

The partnership should continue/not continue because
The partnership would get stronger if the following changes were made/is fine as originally established:

Figure 3.4 Ways to Recognize Partners. *Source*: Adapted from South Washington County School District. (n.d.). Toolkit for building partnerships between schools and business or organization South Washington County Schools. Retrieved from https://docplayer.net/5550265-Toolkit-for-building-partnerships-between-schools-and-businesses-or-organizations-across-south-washington-county-schools.html.

the value of the partnership (South Washington County School District, n.d.). Additional examples of evaluation forms are included in the chapters that follow.

The activity assessment enables you to gather data about the effectiveness of each activity or event associated with the partnership. Several activity assessments contribute to determining the overall success of the partnership. Findings from these assessments also help to shape subsequent initiatives. By the time the annual evaluation is conducted, there should be an overall estimation of the value of the partnership from the feedback given along the way.

Assessment feedback should come from students, teachers, administrative staff, and parents because of the valuable information provided about what is working and what is not. For those not inclined to respond in narrative form, written assessments can include yes-no, multiple choice, or one-word sentence completions. For those not inclined to write at all, conversations and interviews that may or may not be recorded also are very useful feedback mechanisms. Any assessment that is used communicates that the participants' opinions are valued in determining the partnership's worth.

Recognize Partners and Participants Publicly and Privately

Celebrate and honor everyone involved in the partnership. Begin by recognizing the partner and those from the partner institution. Recognition can be as simple as a plaque or banner in the school(s) or as elaborate as a recognition dinner with media coverage. Textbox 3.2 provides a list of ideas to consider, depending on the extent of the partnership and the generosity of the partners.

TEXTBOX 3.2 WAYS TO RECOGNIZE PARTNERS

- Send notes from students to thank partners for their activities
- Have a special place in the school to announce and highlight partnership activities
- Have media coverage by sending news releases and notifying media of special events
- Nominate your partners for district awards
- Recognize partners at appreciation breakfast or luncheon programs
- Include Partners in Education column in the school newsletter
- Share or provide photographs of students and partners working together

- Give partners plaques and banners to thank the partner for their commitment.

Adapted from South Washington County School District. (n.d.). *Toolkit for building partnerships between schools and business or organization South Washington County Schools.* Retrieved from https://docplayer.net/5550265-Toolkit-for-building-partnerships-between-schools-and-businesses-or-organizations-across-south-washington-county-schools.html

Recognition of those involved at the school or district level is equally important because their involvement has given life to the partnership. Public recognition at meetings or events, letters of commendation, certificates of achievement, schedule accommodations, travel vouchers, and monetary gifts are some of the ways in which school-based participants can be rewarded for their efforts to help with the partnership. Any type of recognition contributes to participants' enthusiasm and morale.

REFLECTIONS ON ENTREPRENEURIAL AND STRATEGIC PLANNING FOR PARTNERSHIP ENGAGEMENT

Guidelines for partnerships are as useful as the leader who is using them. Partnership engagement requires individuals at the school and district levels who appreciate the importance of going beyond what exists to get what is needed to reenergize an organization. These individuals do not see roadblocks, but rather envision pathways to possibilities. They are not hampered by naysayers; instead, they pursue opportunities that offer new ideas for educating their students.

The six administrators that you read about in this chapter share these characteristics. They are the "movers and shakers" of our enterprise. They have figured out ways to leverage what they already have to make it even better. They have a can-do, entrepreneurial, open-minded, and positive thinking orientation that propels them to forge ahead.

Justin Aglio from Montour School District said, the "future of education hinges on the strength of partnerships" (Personal Communication, September 20, 2018). These administrators have realized that partnerships add new dimensions to their schools and districts that ultimately enhance their students' learning experiences. They are willing to take that leap and do any extra work that will create pathways to enriching and exciting opportunities.

These administrators appreciate that partnerships are about people and relationships that require hustling, negotiating, and creative thinking (Sanderlin, 2018). They are patient with the process of establishing a shared vision between partners (Sheninger, 2010), yet quick to follow through on responsibilities to keep the momentum going. The next section of this book describes some of the real-life benefits of partnerships with businesses, the community, and colleges and universities.

Part II

REAL-LIFE BENEFITS OF PARTNERSHIPS

Part II describes ways that entrepreneurial leaders can create pathways for partnerships with businesses, the community, and colleges/universities. The first three chapters in this part provide ideas for connecting with the appropriate networks and enlisting stakeholders for each type of partnership. Specific examples of business, community, and college/university partnerships are described in detail for different types of schools. The last chapter discusses critical components for successful partnerships, guidelines for sustaining partnerships, and considerations for renewing those partnerships that work.

Chapter 4

Partnerships with Businesses

Traci Walker Griffith is the principal of the Eliot K-8 Innovation School in Boston, Massachusetts. Traci is a veteran teacher and administrator of the Boston Public Schools. When she became principal of the Eliot, she knew that she had to make a number of changes to help her students make annual yearly progress. In addition to working closely with her teaching staff to change the culture of instruction, she applied to the City of Boston to become an Innovation School so that she would have more flexibility with resources and greater autonomy with budget and staffing.

When Traci started at the Eliot in 2007, she knew that she had to go outside her four walls if she was going to be able to get the resources that her school needed to make transformational changes. Because her school is close to the downtown area, she began to knock on doors to see if there were businesses that would be willing to work with her. She invited people into her school so that they could learn about possible funding opportunities. Traci discovered that she could look to her school's families to help her find and nurture partnerships. Their message to these businesses was that their assistance would help all parts of the community get stronger.

She now has twenty different partnerships that help her school; from a local restaurateur who hosts and donates food and drinks for her school's fund-raising campaign to a local law firm that does pro bono work for the school to Converse® that helps with the school's ice skating event. She has partners who give eyeglasses to children or provide classes on topics such as bookbinding, woodworking, and music education.

Traci believes that public school administrators need to be entrepreneurs to get funding and support. The right partnerships can change the trajectory of a school. She explains that you cannot take "no" for an answer, need to dream big, and think that there always is a way. She explains that a partnership usually will not land in one's lap, but that it is worth the heavy lifting.

Traci has created multiple pathways for connecting with businesses to bring resources to her school. She has used her own entrepreneurial spirit and the commitment of her families to help her make critical connections. Her door-to-door excursions, coupled with her compelling message to businesses to support the future of the economy by enriching children's learning opportunities, are awe inspiring. Most school leaders probably do not have the accessibility, time, or wherewithal to follow Traci's approaches for cultivating partnerships. And, that is okay.

The takeaway from Traci is more about the realization that partnerships with businesses provide human and capital resources that can support teachers' professional development, classroom initiatives, school- and district-wide needs, and community interests that strengthen the overall enterprise of schooling.

REASONS SCHOOL-BUSINESS PARTNERSHIPS WORK

School-business partnerships are a win-win because they help schools with the overall education experience and help businesses with their enhanced goodwill and stronger presence in the community. Partnerships with businesses can improve student motivation and provide students with direction for their future. Such partnerships can offer the following opportunities:

- increased student achievement with mentoring and tutoring programs, in classroom and after-school volunteer programs, science fairs, SAT/ACT training, and scholarship incentive programs
- increased funds for schools with cash returns, fundraising, and materials donations
- increased school to career opportunities with internship programs, field trips to workplaces, job shadowing, and incentive job guarantees
- improved teacher preparation with professional development
- improved product development through teacher feedback (The Council for Corporate & School Partnerships, n.d.a).

When interviewed about their partnerships with businesses, school administrators want to continue because the goals of the partnership and the school are aligned, the partnership is designed to advance the students' educational experience, and the teachers are favorably oriented toward the partnership. School administrators see partnerships with businesses as efforts to advance achievement, provide a needed product or service, improve school facilities or equipment, or generate revenue (The Council for Corporate & School Partnerships, n.d.a).

Business leaders want the partnerships because they want to support schools to improve students' capacity for college and careers. Business leaders believe that schools and businesses have a shared interest and shared responsibility to the community that they serve. Businesses want to provide students with experiences, skills, and a personal vision. However, they do not want to be passive partners who serve as little more than an ATM for initiatives. They want to be engaged in deliberative discussions, interaction, planning, and goal celebration rather than simply playing the role of a resource provider (Badgett, 2016).

USE LOCAL BUSINESS ORGANIZATIONS TO CREATE PATHWAYS TO PARTNERSHIPS

Pathways to business partnerships require an awareness of local business organizations that offer services to schools. This awareness leads to ideas for making connections with specific groups and projects that are pertinent for students of different ages.

U.S. Chamber of Commerce

The U.S. Chamber of Commerce is a membership-based lobbying organization that represents more than three million small and big businesses across the United States providing them with information about policy issues related to business. The Chamber recognizes that it is in the interest of businesses to engage with the education system to have a well-prepared workforce, ready to fill the jobs of tomorrow.

Examples abound with partnerships between local chambers of commerce and school districts. The Richardson, Texas Chamber of Commerce partnered with a local school district to offer high school students a Career and Technical Education course for two hours each week while they work eight hours per week in industries in which they might want to pursue a career. Students do a research project at the end of the course to solve a problem in their chosen industry (Richardson Chamber of Commerce, 2017).

The Rutherford, Tennessee Chamber of Commerce partnered with Central Magnet School in Murfreesboro to provide students with tours of a local hospital's cancer center and manufacturers such as Nissan and Schwann Cosmetics so that they can learn about and make connections in industries that interest them (Murfreesboro News and Radio, 2017). The Rutherford County Chamber of Commerce created Rutherford Works for the county schools to help middle and high school students with career pathways. Included in this array of program opportunities is an externship for middle-school teachers to immerse themselves in STEM-related fields so that they are able to speak from experience as they advise students on educational and career goals (Rutherford County Chamber of Commerce, 2014).

The Chamber of Commerce that serves Middleton, Monroe, and Trenton, Ohio created a Career Ambassadors program for businesses and students. The Chamber established Manufacturing Day to offer tours to local high school students. The Chamber also created Job Exploration for middle-school students by collaborating with Junior Achievement, a nonprofit organization which provides work- and life-based curricula to create "pathways for employability" for students (http://www.thechamberofcommerce.org/education/career-path).

National Federation of Independent Businesses

The National Federation of Independent Businesses (NFIB) is an influential nonpartisan lobbying organization that advocates for small and independent businesses in Washington, DC and in each state capital. Seniors in high school who are entering their freshman year at an accredited two- or four-year university, college, or vocational institute can apply for NFIB's Young Entrepreneur Award Scholarships to win between $2,000 and $15,000.

The 100 scholarships given each year can be applied to tuition or school-related expenses. The seniors must demonstrate entrepreneurial spirit and initiative through having established a business of their own (USAscholarships.com, 2019).

To take advantage of these resources, reach out to your local chapter of the Chamber of Commerce or National Federation of Independent Businesses to become a visible participant to help with networking (The Council for Corporate & School Partnerships, n.d.b.). Also, look to other community organizations that provide networking opportunities for businesspeople. Community organizations such as the Rotary Club, Kiwanis International, and the Lions Club are mentioned in chapter 5.

CONNECT WITH LOCAL BUSINESSES AND ALUMNI

Find ways to connect with small businesses because they represent the largest share of school partners (The Council for Corporate & School Partnerships, n.d.a.). Identify natural business partners, including parents, who might want to become involved. It is important to find out whether they already are engaged in the community or schools, whether they are financially healthy, and the types of causes that are important to them.

Get to know those with whom you personally do business. Discovering a common interest with a storeowner while shopping could present a partnership opportunity. A principal who goes to his local bakery on a weekly basis managed to get the bakery to supply all the baked goods for a senior prom breakfast. In exchange, the baker was able to include "buy one, get one free" coupons in the prom goodie bags. A teacher in another district who has a penchant for her after-school visits to the local chocolate store was able to get the owner to sponsor a field trip each year to the store so that her kindergartners could learn how chocolate is made.

Some local businesses are eager to work with schools, and some are not. Some may have a negative or incorrect perception of what students are like today because of the way in which the media portrays schools. One way to help counter any misperceptions that local businesses have about the schools is to get them into the schools to meet your students. Depending on their expertise and interests, you could invite them to give a short talk to specific classes, be a guest speaker for an assembly, or conduct mock interviews. You also can invite them to attend a student-led event or exhibit, a holiday concert, a special assembly, or an awards ceremony.

Invite them to observe other businesspeople, even their colleagues, mentoring students so that they see firsthand what it is like to volunteer their time. Encourage them to allow job shadowing and internships. Form a local advisory board of school employees, student clubs, parents, and community partners to identify ways to invite local businesspeople into the community (Center for Global Education, 2018).

Reach Out to Alumni

Alumni, especially those who have been honored by the school for their achievements and contributions, often are likely to give back to their schools in the form of donations, scholarships, and services. One principal shared that one of his alumni established a scholarship for his high school students to help them financially with their four years of college. This alumnus, now a lawyer, worked with the principal to establish a series of experiences for the high school students to take field trips to lower Manhattan to understand the history of the financial district and engage in summer internships at his law firm. He also participated in mock trials and career day at the high school, and all for free.

This principal shared that so many of his relationships with alumni and local businesses depended on his willingness and wherewithal to pursue opportunities that had potential yet required work. These partnerships had to be mutually beneficial. He needed to have an open mind, be flexible, and empower and support those willing to engage in a partnership (Sheninger, 2010).

CORE VALUES FOR WORKING WITH BUSINESSES

Partnerships with businesses should be in place to provide educational opportunities and programs to support student achievement. Partnerships need to be aligned with the strategic plan and core values of the district. Open and ongoing communication between parties will contribute to ensuring that the partnership goals, which support the school's and district's strategic plan and core values, are realized (South Washington County School District, n.d.).

Administrator's View on Partnerships and Core Values

Justin Aglio who is Director of Academic Achievement and District Innovation at Montour School District in Pittsburgh, Pennsylvania has been involved in forming many business partnerships on behalf of his district. He works with his district's teachers, administrators, and board members to develop partnership opportunities that foster the district's mission of putting children first. He knows that his teachers must take ownership because they are the ones who will be most directly involved with whatever comes the district's way. He also knows that, while the district values partnerships, he will not pursue partnerships that do not support the curriculum, help his teachers, or promote students' learning needs.

Among the many partnerships that Justin helped his district to form is one with LEGO Education, as briefly described in chapter 2. Justin received a call from the President of LEGO North America to see if Montour wanted to build the first official LEGO classroom in the schools. He and his colleagues decided that students' experiences in designing a classroom and building furniture for the room out of LEGOs would be a tremendous learning experience. He and his team worked many months to develop a mutually beneficial partnership with LEGO Education. Justin and his colleagues designed the room and then worked with his community to get grants and donations for enough LEGOs to build this innovative room, which the teachers now use.

Justin also spoke excitedly about a partnership with the Fred Rogers Center as an example of how so much of partnership work is voluntary. A small group of first-grade teachers began to look at how they interact with their students when technology is present. They had to videotape themselves and make a list of best practices. Word spread about the possibilities with this project with all the first-grade teachers. By the next day, he received an email from the teachers that they all wanted to participate. In exchange, they were able to tour the Fred Rogers Center (go to http://www.fredrogerscenter.org/ for more information).

Justin believes that, for partnerships to work, school leaders need to be adaptable and nimble with new ideas. At the same time, school leaders need to stay true to their core values, make sure students are at the center of partnerships with businesses, be aware of and responsive to community needs, and make sure that everything that they do is ethical. He is aware that sometimes people partner because it looks nice on the outside, but he knows that such partnerships do not work.

COMMERCIALISM IN THE SCHOOLS

Even with the benefits mentioned above, the idea of school-business partnerships is somewhat controversial because of possible commercialism in the schools. Much has been written about the intended and unintended consequences of corporate influences on educational systems (Coburn & McCafferty, 2016). Whenever a school or district forms a relationship with a business that provides access to students or staff in exchange for fiscal or in-kind resources (i.e., goods or services), commercialism often is a by-product of such an affiliation.

Businesses might sponsor school activities (e.g., sporting events), get naming rights by building football stadiums or parts of athletic fields, provide access to products that include electronic marketing, donate products for fundraising (e.g., candy sales), or sponsor educational materials. Businesses might donate computer equipment and other educational products to schools with the requirement that students spend time listening to or viewing advertisements.

Criticisms proliferate when business vendors push to form partnerships with schools to appeal to captive students who are susceptible to the products advertised. Critics charge that school-based commercialism is the corruption of public education because it needlessly subjects children to unhealthy products and promotions. There are even claims that such marketing activities promote unwholesome behaviors that contribute to, for instance, the childhood obesity epidemic in America (Brent & Lunden, 2009; McCollum, 2005; Molnar, 2003; Pennington, 2005; Shaw, 2000; Viadero, 2009).

There have been efforts to restrict or set limits to commercialism in schools. The National Parent Teacher Association (PTA) adopted a set of guidelines years ago to limit corporate involvement in education. These guidelines, which communicated parents' outspoken concerns about business practices in schools, confined business partnerships to education-related projects and barred advertising from the classroom (Weisman, 1991).

Much depends on the type and purpose of the partnership that is formed. There is a big difference in forming a school-business partnership that focuses on mentoring students by corporate employees versus one that is solely about the in-school plugging of products. Recommendations from the National Association of Secondary School Principals (NASSP) (2002) include the need to consider the "spectrum of giving" when deciding whether to embrace a business partnership.

Ask the "tough questions" to determine the ratio of benefits to the company versus the school and students. As you make decisions, consider the political climate. Be aware of what has worked and failed in the past (The Council for Corporate & School Partnerships, n.d.a.). Seek insight from other individuals and groups that have engaged in business education partnerships.

Many business partnerships offer districts a much needed means to supplement their resources or an educational product that contributes significantly to teachers' pedagogical toolbox (Hogan, Enright, Stylianou, & McCuaig, 2018; Kaplan, 1996).

You can and should find the right balance between corporate support and commercial infringement with the presence of advertising in schools. After all, a lack of funding for strong educational programs motivates you to look for sources of support from businesses, especially those that can enhance educational quality and be a good neighbor in the process. Do your homework about the quid pro quo value of potential school-business partnerships (Engeln, 2003).

Confirm that learning resources, technology tools, and student experiences are worth it before accepting any proposal. Weigh the value of free products (e.g., software, posters, and websites) in relation to a business's expectations. Safeguard the autonomy of your students and ensure that their developing values are not influenced by corporate sponsorships (Brighouse, 2005; Carr, 2010).

Work with your community to make wise decisions regarding corporate involvement, especially in determining when advertising can play a constructive role in your school or district (Moore, 2007). Communicate and illustrate to your community the many benefits and characteristics of effective partnerships (Daily, Swain, Huysman, & Tarrant, 2010).

When relationships with businesses build upon a shared understanding of values and culture to support mutual needs, and offer long-term, sustainable benefits for students and schools, true partnerships begin to exist. Just as schools have widely diverse needs, so do businesses. It is up to both entities to learn from the successful efforts of others and create new opportunities that ultimately benefit students (The Council for Corporate & School Partnerships, n.d.a.).

PARTNERSHIPS FOR FUND RAISING

Businesses do not necessarily require official partnerships with schools to provide benefits to students. There are opportunities from local and national businesses and corporations that provide incentives to customers to use their purchases to give back to local schools.

Stop and Shop's A+ School Rewards Program

Stop and Shop's A+ School Rewards Program, begun in 2005, is an example of such a program that appeals to its customers to bring back money to their local schools. Customers can support up to two schools to benefit from their A+ School Rewards that accrue with each purchase. Customers create an online account with a Stop & Shop card number to keep track of their points earned.

Schools must sign up to participate in the program. A principal, whose signature is required, and a coordinator get an ID number that customers use to give points to the school. At the end of each month, the points earned are used in a calculation to determine a school's cash total, which is then automatically credited to the school's account. When schools receive a check, they can decide the best way to use the funds, whether for the purchase of computers, smart boards, educational materials, or field trips. This school-business opportunity is a great way for principals to involve their Parent Teacher Associations (PTA).

Examples of PTAs that are involved with this fund-raising initiative are Madison Middle School in Trumbull, Connecticut (https://www.trumbullps.org/mms/pta/pta-info/31-programs-that-give-back.html), Hindley School in Darien, Connecticut (http://www.hindleypto.org/stop-shop-a-rewards/), Avon Intermediate School in West Grove, PA (http://www.agispta.org/), and PS/IS 217 on Roosevelt Island, New York (https://www.217pta.com/a-rewards-program.html). These PTAs use their web pages to communicate to their parent community reasons and procedures for participation.

Pursuing Fundraising Opportunities

One way to find local and national fundraising programs is to search for school rewards programs. PTAs should run the right programs, and not too many, so that they are not accused of fundraising overkill and have enough volunteers who are willing to help with what they perceive to be a valuable program. There are articles that provide guidance on the programs to run. One such article rates fund-raising opportunities with a Work-Reward-Attention Equation. This equation evaluates the amount of work it takes to run a program in relation to the amount of reward a group can expect to receive and the amount of promotional work that is done by the sponsoring company (Sullivan, 2018).

Table 4.1 provides information about four corporate fundraising programs and ways in which schools have used these opportunities. The names and rules of these incentive programs might change.

Table 4.1 Corporate Fund-Raising Opportunities for Schools

Company	Name of Program	How Program Works	Eligible Schools	Examples of Uses and Outcomes
Office Depot Sells supplies and products	**Give Back to Schools**	• Consumers purchase qualifying school supplies and provide school ID at checkout (in store and online) • Designated school receives 5 percent back in merchandise credit for free supplies at Office Depot and Office Max • Office Depot has teamed up with the National PTA to cultivate this program • For information, go to https://www.officedepot.com/cm/school-supplies/give-back	Public and private P–12 schools	Santa Rita Elementary School Los Altos, CA https://santaritaschool.org/santaritaes/6999-Fundraising.html#officedepot Litchfield Middle School Litchfield, IL http://lms.lcusd12.org/easy-fundraising.html Maui High School Kahului, HI https://www.mauihigh.org/apps/news/show_news.jsp?REC_ID=464052&id=5
Office Depot	**School Supply Drive**	• Consumers purchase extra supplies and place them in collection boxes in their neighborhood Office Depot and Office Max retail stores to give to schools • For information, go to https://www.marketwatch.com/press-release/office-depot-helps-thousands-of-students-and-teachers-go-back-to-school-proud-this-year-2018-10-01	Title I schools	More than 1,000 schools have received school supplies

(*Continued*)

Table 4.1 Corporate Fund-Raising Opportunities for Schools (*Continued*)

Company	Name of Program	How Program Works	Eligible Schools	Examples of Uses and Outcomes
Office Depot	**Start Proud!**	• Office Depot associates host backpack bundling bashes in local markets where they fill 20,000 backpacks, valued collectively at more than $1 million, with back-to-school essentials such as notebooks, folders, pencils, and glue • The backpacks are distributed to students at the beginning of the school year during ten celebratory assemblies nationwide • Office Depot, in partnership with Boise Paper and Domtar Paper, also provide pallets of school supplies to teachers at each of the ten schools • For information, go to https://www.youtube.com/watch?v=y0ufqci9vNY	Title I schools	One "All-Star" educator is recognized at each Start Proud! assembly with approximately $1,000 worth of premium supplies, including computers and classroom furniture
General Mills Sells food products	**Box Tops for Education**	• Parents and community members clip box top coupons on more than 100 General Mills and other brands (e.g., Ziploc, Hefty, Kleenex, and Scott) and send them to their school. The school redeems them at ten cents per coupon • Schools must be registered and have an ID code • The school's program coordinator submits all collected box top coupons • Checks are issued two times each year • Schools can purchase anything they need; computers, books, and playground equipment • For information, go to https://www.boxtops4education.com/about	K–8 schools	Northwest Elementary Tampa, FL *Covered playground and garden* Vanguard Elementary Denver, CO *New school library* Black Hawk Education Center East Moline, IL *New playground* More examples at https://www.boxtops4education.com/Videos/

(*Continued*)

Table 4.1 Corporate Fund-Raising Opportunities for Schools (*Continued*)

Company	Name of Program	How Program Works	Eligible Schools	Examples of Uses and Outcomes
Coca Cola Sells beverages	**Coca Cola Give**	• Consumers scan codes from Coca Cola products to donate to a school of their choosing • Coca Cola provides a toolkit for schools to get the word out. The toolkit includes branded marketing flyers but gives specific instructions about responsible advertising to avoid presenting or giving marketing materials to children • For information, go to https://us.coca-cola.com/give/	**K-12 public and private schools**	Briarmeadow Charter School Houston, TX http://briarmeadowpto.digitalpto.com/fundraising/affinity-programs/coca-cola-gives/ North Delta School Batesville, MS http://www.northdeltaschool.net/Support-NDS Saint Helen Catholic School South Bend, IN https://stasb.org/rewards
Amazon Sells products and services online	**Amazon Associates Program**	• Schools that join become an "Associate" • Schools earn money for sales from web traffic of school referrals to Amazon through special links on the school's website and social media • Schools get a certain percentage for different products purchased • Instead of going directly to Amazon, consumers click on the school or district's link • Consumers get the same Amazon purchase price but earn referral fees for the school or district • For information, go to https://affiliate-program.amazon.com/	**P-12 public and private schools**	Mountain View School Santa Barbara, CA http://www.mtnview.goleta.k12.ca.us/pta/amazon/ South Layette School District McDonald, PA https://www.southfayette.org/domain/334 New Haven School District Union City, CA https://www.mynhusd.org/apps/pages/index.jsp?uREC_ID=414974&type=d&pREC_ID=905710

PARTNERSHIPS WITH PRODUCT DONATIONS

Partnerships with businesses can involve donations to incentivize students to perform at higher levels and function better to receive needed tools and resources. While the examples that follow may not be geographically feasible for your school or district, they can provide ideas for business partnerships to possibly pursue for your own region.

Partnerships to Promote Attendance

The Tustin Unified School District (TUSD) in Tustin, California formed a partnership with Toshiba to promote perfect attendance by students across the district. Toshiba donated thirty laptop computers to the district. One laptop is given away at the end of the academic year to every elementary, middle, and high school in TUSD. Called Toshiba Perfect Attendance Program, all students who maintain perfect daily attendance have a chance to win the laptop. The district's goal is to have every child in every seat every day. A sample message to the parent community can be found at https://www.tustin.k12.ca.us/heritage/resources/forms-and-policies/toshiba-perfect-attendance-program.

This district also is partnering with Tustin Toyota to increase overall student attendance by highlighting high school seniors who model exemplary attendance and achievement. Called Tustin Toyota: "Drive for Perfect Attendance" Program, all seniors who maintain perfect daily attendance at one of the four high schools are eligible to enter a lottery for a brand-new Toyota Corolla. The winning student is presented with the vehicle at his or her graduation ceremony (Beckman High School, n.d.).

Partnerships to Promote Students' Eyesight

Warby Parker, a New York-based company that sells glasses and sunglasses, created the Pupils Project for K-8 Students in New York City and Baltimore Public Schools. When the Warby team conducted an analysis of vision care in the United States, they realized that children, especially those from low income and minority backgrounds, needed access to vision care. They worked with the New York City and Baltimore governments and school districts to form a partnership to administer free vision screenings, eye exams, and glasses.

Warby Parker's medical partners administer vision screenings and eye exams in the children's classrooms, and Warby provides the glasses, which each student handpicks from a trunk setup at the school. As the Warby Parker founders share, this is their first pair of glasses for so many students. Johns Hopkins University is conducting research to understand the correlation between the intervention of vision treatment and reading scores (Warby Parker, n.d.).

Partnerships for Teachers' Professional Development

Jeanette Schulz works for Amgen Foundation as the lead for K-12 STEM Initiatives. She vows, and rightfully so, for her company's good will with schools to form partnerships to enhance teachers' professional development. Amgen is a multinational biopharmaceutical company headquartered in Thousand Oaks, California that is focused on discovering medicines for patients with serious illnesses. Her company's outreach to schools began when two Amgen scientists decided that they wanted to improve science education for students by providing access to biotechnology resources to high school teachers.

These scientists worked with a biology teacher in California in 1989 to develop a series of labs to bring to high school classrooms. At that time, Amgen also agreed to give these classrooms equipment and supplies for the labs in area high schools.

The program has grown to reach almost 90,000 students and 1,500 teachers each year in different parts of the United States, Canada, Europe, Australia, and Asia. Today, known as the Amgen Biotech Experience, the program empowers teachers to bring biotechnology into their classrooms by providing them with the necessary professional development, teaching materials, and research-grade lab equipment. Principal Melanie Welsh, mentioned in chapter 1, brought this program to her high school at no cost.

Jeanette Schulz explained that, through this program, teachers volunteer to participate—attending professional development institutes to learn the curriculum and embedding the content in their existing biology and biotechnology courses. Over the past almost thirty years, teachers have come back again and again to deliver this program to their students as they see the value that it provides in both creating high-quality learning experiences for their students with the use of research-grade scientific equipment and opening doors to help students see potential opportunities in science.

The program's website (http://www.amgenbiotechexperience.com/impact-stories) speaks to ways in which this program has transformed teachers' and students' lives.

PARTNERSHIPS WITH EMPLOYEE VOLUNTEERISM

There are businesses that truly want to engage their employees in volunteerism in the schools. It could include single or multiple days of service or short-term or long-term mentoring.

Service to the Schools

The Entrepreneurs Foundation of Central Texas brings companies together to help with various service activities that benefit local elementary schools. These service days bring together member companies and their team members to volunteer. One such event takes place in two elementary schools, Brooke and Linder of the Austin Independent School District in Texas. Twenty-three companies, including Austin Ventures, BestFit Mobile, mindSHIFT Technologies, and NVIDIA, meet at the schools for a Spring Service Day to mulch, build a running track, prune bushes, create gardens, and paint to improve campus grounds.

Nvidia, an information technology corporation in Santa Clara, California, created its own Project Inspire to encourage its employees to participate in service activities around the world. An important focus of many of their activities has been the schools. Employees from its Austin, Texas office have gone to Pecan Springs Elementary School in Austin Independent School District to build a sustainable garden to improve science education and provide fresh produce for low-income families (Nvidia, n.d.).

Employees from Nvidia's Beaverton, Oregon office beautified Aloha High School, an under-resourced school, by prepping and painting hallways and removing graffiti, power-washing around its campus, and improving the main athletic field's press box and restrooms. Employees at Nvidia's Westford, Massachusetts office partnered with the nearby Bartlett Community Partnership School to build benches and shelving, paint murals, and landscape outdoor spaces. The office also donated two NVIDIA Jetson TX1 SE kits to help students gain firsthand experience for robotics projects (Nvidia, n.d.).

Keenan & Associates, a broker/consultant firm that addresses insurance needs for California schools, community colleges, public agencies, and hospitals, has been recognized as a leader in corporate social responsibility. All Keenan employees are involved with schools and communities. They have a day each year where all employees work on projects for their local nonprofits. One such project includes preparing back-to-school backpacks for youth or good night kits for homeless children (Keenan & Associates, 2019).

Keenan teamed up with Association of California School Administrators to create the Everyday Kindness program to promote kindness in the classroom and communities. School boards actually pass a resolution to participate in this program (https://everyday-kindness.secure.force.com/apex/toolkit). Tools are made available to schools to identify, record, and celebrate everyday acts of kindness. Approximately 100 schools across 50 school districts in California are participating (Keenan & Associates, 2019).

Mentoring

MENTOR, a national mentoring partnership, promotes the importance of mentoring young people, especially those from low-income areas, to help them stay in school and possibly go to college. This organization has done a great deal of research on the significant positive effects of mentoring on students' school attendance and college enrollment (MENTOR: The National Mentoring Partnership, 2019).

This organization works with businesses to develop mentoring relationships that help students and contribute to employee satisfaction and productivity. Two companies which are part of this group, Luxottica and Ernst & Young, are described below.

Mentoring High School Students. Withrow High School in Cincinnati, Ohio formed a number of partnerships, one of which is with Luxottica. This international company designs, manufactures, and distributes eyewear. Each year, forty-five Withrow High School students in grades 9–12 are paired with Luxottica employees who mentor them throughout high school. Mentees and mentors meet monthly at one of Luxottica's offices. Students receive valuable one-on-one time with their mentors and attend professional development courses (Luxottica, 2014).

Seniors can apply for one of four $4,000 college scholarships, which encourages them to seek education beyond high school. In 2012, Luxottica, in partnership with Cincinnati Public Schools and other organizations, expanded their support of Withrow High School students to provide laptops and charging stations for the eleventh- and twelfth-grade students and faculty to provide support for technology-based initiatives (Luxottica, 2014).

Mentoring for College. Although specific partnerships do not exist between schools and Ernst & Young, schools can collaborate to identify some of their underserved high school students who have potential to succeed in college. Ernst & Young's College MAP (Mentoring for Access and Persistence) program is a signature volunteer program that targets underserved high school students who have the potential to succeed in college. Ernst & Young, a global accounting firm, began a program called College MAP (Mentoring for Access and Persistence). Employees work with high schools to identify juniors and seniors who need extra help in preparing for college.

After graduating from high school, these students or College MAP Collegians enter the Persistence stage of the program. They participate in periodic in-person gatherings as well as monthly webinars on topics of immediate relevance. One of the pilot high schools for this program, Martin Luther King Jr. Early College Preparatory High in Denver, Colorado, has students who have gained access to college because of the skills that they learned (EY, n.d.).

Mentoring Middle-School Students. The investment firm Capital Group partnered with Sul Ross Middle School of Northside Independent School District in San Antonio, Texas to create "It's All About the Students." This three-year mentoring program, which begins in sixth grade, helps middle school students develop academically and socially.

Almost 100 Capital Group employees volunteer in the school as mentors and assistants. Capital Group even provides university scholarships to students who meet specific criteria. As mentioned in chapter 1, this same investment group provides office supplies for teachers, school supplies for students, and funds for field trips in the middle school. The middle-school administrators believe that the support and passion by the Capital Group employees have been invaluable for the students (Northside Independent School District, 2015).

PARTNERSHIPS TO SUPPORT SECONDARY STUDENTS' CAREER READINESS

The Cristo Rey Jesuit High School of Milwaukee, Wisconsin established a Corporate Work Study Program (CWSP) so that their students have hands-on, professional work experience with local companies. Students work in job-sharing teams of four and work five full days per month within normal business hours. Students can work without missing any classes.

Students are employees of a separately incorporated CWSP, which the sponsoring organization pays quarterly, annually, or monthly for the services of the students. Students perform a range of entry-level work from administrative to research. The income that the students receive helps to pay for a portion of their educational costs. Cristo Rey has more than seventy partners, with local businesses being a major source of work opportunities for students (Cristo Rey Jesuit, 2016).

American Transmission Company (ATC), a multistate, transmission-only utility in the United States, is one of the school's partners. Students at ATC work on entry-level tasks in several departments: information technology, human resources, facilities, real estate, environmental and system operations support. ATC believes that the students gain valuable experience in professional work environments, and ATC benefits from their help, especially in developing the area's talent pool for the future (American Transition Company, 2018).

High School Career Academy's Approach to Partnerships

The Information Technology (IT) Career Academy in an urban community in a southeastern state sought and nurtured support from the business community from the onset of the school's existence. The founding principal developed a position for a career specialist to serve as the lynchpin between the school and the business community. This career specialist has used a grassroots approach to reach out to businesses to help the academy's students become career ready.

Business partners support student clubs, help with fundraising and donations, serve as mentors, provide teacher training, participate in career awareness events, allow job shadowing, and provide paid internships. The paid internships are especially noteworthy because, regardless of the company's size, the academy's high school seniors have authentic progressive work during the summer for eight to ten weeks. These paid interns get real-world and challenging experiences.

This career specialist also has formed a Business Advisory Council that consists of seventy members with approximately twenty to twenty-five members of the council attending the meetings in person on a regular basis. The remainder of the members call into the meeting via conference call. Council members also have a spring mixer and summer retreat. Council members have a common purpose with goals and a strong sense of identity that is supported by CEOs, vice presidents, and other key stakeholders in the IT community. They establish priorities for their engagement with the academy and its students. They are a robust network of large corporations, midsize employers, and small businesses (Hernandez-Gantes, Brookins, & Fletcher, 2017).

GUIDELINES FOR FORMING PARTNERSHIPS WITH BUSINESSES

This chapter's examples of successful school-business partnerships reflect the enthusiastic determination and know-how of the partnership stakeholders. There is an entrepreneurial spirit for crafting opportunities for schools and students. The seven guidelines that follow incorporate many of the ideas and behaviors that have enabled these partnerships to flourish. Textbox 4.1 provides highlights of the guidelines.

TEXTBOX 4.1 GUIDELINES FOR FORMING BUSINESS PARTNERSHIPS

1. Adhere to the three golden rules of partnerships: *relationships, communication,* and *responsiveness*
2. Identify common ground as you engage businesses
3. Remember that you must "Give to Get"

4. Develop a Business Advisory Council
5. Be prepared for changes in leadership
6. Secure documented support at the highest level
7. Determine your role in forming partnerships.

1. Adhere to the three golden rules of partnerships: *relationships, communication,* and *responsiveness*.

   Partnerships with businesses are all about cultivating ongoing and fruitful *relationships* with those in positions to tap into their resources to bring to the schools. Business owners and business leaders need to know that they and their products and services are valued and appreciated. School and district leaders need to ensure that they have positive relationships with their own community of stakeholders so that they are receptive to businesses coming into their schools.

   As leaders "in the middle" of negotiating opportunities between businesses and their schools, they know that they must form and sustain positive and productive relationships with authority figures and other interested parties who can help partnerships come to fruition.

   Communication solidifies relationships with stakeholders. Business owners and leaders must be involved with the partnerships' intended goals, activities, and outcomes. Someone from the school community should be communicating with them frequently, honestly, and openly. School-based personnel and the community need the same courtesy extended to them about ongoing activities and outcomes. Communication mechanisms can be personal letters, website updates, newsletters, email, posters and flyers, and oral presentations.

   Responsiveness communicates the authenticity of the relationship. When business owners or leaders know that someone in the school or district is available on a regular basis to work on the partnership, they develop an appreciation for their partners. It is all about forging a relationship that is built on trust and a positive attitude.

2. Identify common ground as you engage businesses. Identify an effective approach to use to reach out to businesses so that you are not too aggressive or too bashful. Try to strike the right chord with those you meet. Check on the motivation of potential business partners. Engage local businesses by inviting them to your school to be a guest speaker, attend student exhibits, mentor, or conduct mock interviews. Encourage them to allow job shadowing and internships. Form a local advisory board of teachers, students, parents, and community partners to find ways to invite local businesspeople into the schools (Center for Global Education, 2018).

   Establish common ground for the partnership by understanding how the business's motivation for forming the partnership fits with the values of the community and the goals for students. If the community does not support advertising or merchandizing on school grounds, do not pursue this type of partnership. Use research about previously successful partnerships, parent surveys, or potential business partners' presentations before PTA groups to help determine the viability of partnerships for your school or district (The Council for Corporate & School Partnerships, n.d.b.).

3. Keep in mind the very nature of quid pro quo, and don't be afraid of "giving to get" because the "get" might be very beneficial for your teachers and students. Business philanthropy and altruism are not the only reasons for school engagement. Businesses also want to boost some facet of their enterprise, whether it is employee morale, employee recruitment and retention, increased publicity, revenue, or customer loyalty (The Council for Corporate & School Partnerships, n.d.a.).

To reap the benefits of the partnership—whether it is through services, products, or cash—be fully aware that something in return will be expected. It could be private recognition with emails, telephone calls, and letters, or public recognition with appreciation meals, website announcements, or media coverage. It could be student and parent exposure to advertising or joint sponsorships of events that promote the business. Or, it could be a business's involvement in creating policies and procedures for student learning. Prior to forming any official partnership, determine your level of tolerance for what you and your school community are willing to give back.

4. Consider the idea of developing a Business Advisory Council. If your school needs require multiple business partnerships to provide services and products to students (e.g., a theme-based magnet school or career-oriented secondary school), form an advisory council of local businesspeople, community members, and school personnel to establish common ground for the partnerships.

The IT Career Academy mentioned above used such a council as a grassroots organization to establish a shared mission and set of goals for business involvement in this school. The council's regularly scheduled meetings and social events, led by a school-based administrator, resulted in buy-in by all stakeholders. A business advisory council, if comprised of the right people and run well, offers direction, purpose, and commitment to the partnerships.

5. Understand that leadership changes are inevitable. Many great partnerships existed in the past, but either the school leader or business leader left. The partnership ended with the change in leadership. If your predecessor had partnerships that flourished, do what you can to continue with them. Seek multiple perspectives on the value of previously existing partnerships. Work to understand the breadth and depth of support from teachers, parents, and students.

This will contribute to your own formulation of plans on how to proceed. If the business leader no longer works for the company, do what you

can to find someone else to continue with the partnership. In addition to reaching out through emails and letters, go in person or send a designee to meet with the new business leader or liaison. The same applies to small businesses that continue to exist, but with different owners. New business employees and new owners might not know about the partnership and could be quite enthusiastic about starting anew.
6. Secure explicit support for the partnership within your school and district. The partnership should have support at the highest level. The superintendent and school board should articulate and demonstrate support for the partnership internally and externally so that it is taken seriously. Insist on a paper trail of support, whether with MOUs, emails, or memoranda. Teachers, employees, and other constituents should support the partnerships.

    Ideally, their support is requested and given before official documents are signed so that they feel that they have a voice in the decision-making. The parent community should have the opportunity to review and contribute to partnerships so that they too believe that their input matters. Expect that, even with efforts to garner broad support, there will be individuals and groups that have issues with impending partnerships. Although not ideal, the most important documented support must come from those fiscally and legally responsible for the district.
7. Determine whether you are the best person to pursue business partnerships. This means that you have the interest, time, patience, and wherewithal to invest in forming and sustaining relationships with individuals in the business community. If not, identify someone who can serve as your designee to carry out the role. An administrator or teacher who works alone or works with you to develop the partnerships can be your designee.

    Alternatively, you could identify a team of individuals beyond yourself; one person who excels at outreach and another who excels at communication and follow through.

    With any configuration, empower your colleague or colleagues to do whatever is needed to identify and approach potential business partners that support the school or district's core values. Make sure that you are kept in the loop if you are not part of a team. Cultivate a strong bond with your PTA so that it can help with the fund-raising aspect of working with businesses. Make sure that the PTA also keeps you apprised of its efforts and outcomes.

CREATING OPPORTUNITIES WITH BUSINESSES

If business partnerships can offer additional learning tools, assistance with health and well-being, experiences with adults who can serve as important role models, tutoring or mentoring, exciting field trips, or career development opportunities at little or no financial or ethical cost to the community, it behooves you to pursue such opportunities. With a mindset that businesses can enrich your school or district, you have a chance to establish new relationships that are energizing and valuable. Although some partnerships can create challenges, the key is to "stay committed and focused across the ups and downs, and you will succeed" (The Council for Corporate & School Partnerships, n.d.a, p. 21).

Chapter 5

Partnerships with Communities

"It takes a village." This refrain, while sometimes overused, is the mantra of principal Cassandra Lewis Davis of DeKalb County, Georgia. It has real meaning and optimizes her work in her school. As a new principal, Cassandra walked into a far too typical situation—a failing school with a persistent academic achievement gap in a community of need in several areas—food insecurity, housing insecurity, and job insecurity. Her students needed help; her parents needed help. With a background in social services and special education, Cassandra understood the importance of addressing the social and emotional welfare of her students as well as the academics.

The lives of her students outside of school affect what happens in school. She realized she needed to support and help her students' families in order to help improve her school and the academic success of her students. Cassandra believes that students and their families *"can't live apart from community."* So, she brought the community to the school. She sponsored a Think Tank breakfast.

Cassandra reached out to the stakeholders of her community. She invited local clergy, businesses, service organizations, civil organizations, members of sororities and fraternities, government agencies, and the school board to the Think Tank Breakfast. With all the members in one room, breaking bread, she told her story. As a team they assessed the needs of the school and its community. She identified what the members of the community, agencies, and organizations could do to address the needs of her school and its community.

Before addressing the status of academics in her school, Cassandra addressed the community issues and leveraged partnerships with the members of her Think Tank. The school building was in disrepair. The abandoned buildings, transitional housing, and garbage and trash the students had to walk past in order to go to school affected how the students felt about school.

Through the partnerships developed from the members of the Think Tank improvements began.

The Board of Education repaired their building maintenance issues. The city enforced code violations related to garbage and trash accumulated in abandoned homes. Churches provided food and clothing to those students and their families experiencing food and housing insecurities. Children began to feel comfortable coming to school. Now, academics could begin.

CREATE PATHWAYS FOR COMMUNITY PARTNERSHIPS

"Something mysterious happens when community involvement contributes to improvement in student achievement . . . meaningful community involvement sets in motion a chain of events that transforms the culture of the school, and often, the community the school servers" (Hatch, 1998, p. 16). Community organizations, agencies, and individual members have a stake in supporting their local schools. As schools are an integral part of a community, all members of the community play a part in the success of their most vulnerable members of the community—the children.

As with creating a pathway to business partnerships described in chapter 4, school and district leaders need to know what their community agencies and individuals can offer as support through partnerships. This is exactly what Cassandra did. Her invitation to a Think Tank Breakfast created a path to a multitude of partnerships that bettered the chances of the students in her school, their families, and the community at large.

School leaders seek community partnerships for several reasons; however, improving student academic achievement and student success are most common. Student success is primary and essential (Epstein, 2010; Sanders & Lewis, 2005). Other interrelated reasons include supporting and improving school quality and its education and collaborating with the community's overall development (Sanders & Lewis, 2005).

Most community agencies and organizations have a mission that involves service in some capacity. Community members share interest, concern, and responsibility for their youth. Many of these organizations have developed networks of multiple partnerships that have grown from local grassroots initiatives to national entities.

As you set out to create pathways for community partnerships, expand the notion of what *community* means. Expand the definition of community to reach beyond the local neighborhood of the students to any neighborhood that could impact their schooling and development. Expand community to include not just groups with social and economic status, but also individuals with talents and strengths to share with youth. Expand community to include all members of the community, not just those who have children in the schools (Epstein, 2010).

There are several types of community organizations and agencies that entrepreneurial school leaders can tap to form partnerships; for example, government and military, national service, health care, faith-based, cultural and recreational, senior citizen, and college/university. Three levels of potential community partnership are national organizations, local organizations and agencies, and individual community members (Sanders, 2001).

COMMUNITY SCHOOLS

The websites and documents of the Children's Aid Society, the National Center for Community Schools, the Coalition of Community Schools, and the Institute for Educational Leadership provide a wealth of information related to the mission, implementation, and sustainability of community schools. Whether or not a school becomes a full-fledged community school or only has a couple of community partnerships, the information from these organizations can help develop a plan and forge a path to engaging school-community partnerships.

A community school (sometimes referred to as full-service community school or community learning center) is the hub of a constellation of partnerships (business, community, and/or college/university) to meet the needs of its students and their families. The partnerships are collocated in the school and offer a range of services that "provide expanded learning opportunities that are motivating and engaging during the school day, after school, and in the summer, and offer essential health and social supports and services" (Coalition for Community Schools at the Institute for Educational Leadership, 2009b, para 2–3).

Community schools are different from regular or traditional schools in their transformational intentionality, goals, and structure. They see their relationships with the community, its members, organizations, and institutions as learning resources that are mutually beneficial to all. Community schools strive to reduce the challenges students bring to school and build social capital for their students and their families. There usually is a community school coordinator who aligns the partnership work with school goals and initiatives (Coalition for Community Schools at the Institute for Educational Leadership, 2009b).

According to the Coalition of Community Schools (Community Schools at the Institute for Educational Leadership, 2009b), there are six key conditions of learning that a community school must address for every child to succeed.

These six conditions are fulfilled through the working partnership between the school and its community:

- nurturing, high quality early childhood comprehensive programs
- qualified teachers who have high expectations, high standards, and a challenging curriculum
- motivated, engaged students in school and in the community
- response to the physical, emotional, and mental needs of students and their families
- collaboration and mutual respect among school personnel, families, and parents
- promotion of a safe school climate that engages the community and the broader learning community.

A hallmark of a community school is the focus on providing experiences that match the needs of students, their families, and their community. There are four focus areas:

- learning experiences that go beyond the classroom walls and school calendar
- support and services in the areas of health and social well-being
- engaging families and the community
- early childhood development support.

As such, each community school will look different as the needs and goals are local and individual (Coalition of Community Schools at the Institute for Educational Leadership, 2009b).

Community schools seek to develop partnerships to provide round-the-clock learning. Based on the idea that learning does not stop at the end of the school day and the learning experiences and learning opportunities exist beyond school walls and the school calendar, community schools seek to provide engaging curriculum in school through partnerships with community art and cultural groups, local businesses, community service organizations, and local institutions of higher education (Santiago, Ferrara, & Quinn, 2012).

Opportunities for learning out-of-school time (OST) are nurtured through the expansion of the school day by offering after-school programs that connect and link with the school curriculum. Programs are developed and offered during the summer and school vacations; thus, extending and expanding the curriculum as well as combating the typical summer slide in academic achievement.

Entrepreneurial leaders seek community-based organizations (CBOs) to support programs in school and OST that focus on youth development to promote college and career aspirations, prepare good citizens for the future, and encourage relationships with peers and adults. Examples of activities for youth development are mentoring programs, student advocacy groups, and conflict resolution training. These programs recognize youth's assets and potential while they guide them to develop skills and strengths.

A Bit of History

The Children's Aid Society (CAS) of New York has been invested in the success of poverty-stricken children and their families for more than 150 years. They provide a network of services to almost 5,000 families in more than 50 sites in New York City. Their primary goal is to create and support stable families. Once home stability is established through housing, health care, and counseling assistance, children have a better chance of focusing on learning. Children can participate in a myriad of programs the CAS supports: continued health care, academic programs, sport programs, and art programs (Children's Aid, 2019).

At one time, the CAS only served New York City. Now they are a model for other agencies and have spin-off organizations that network nationally and internationally. In 1992, the CAS took the next step by forming their first set of partnerships with New York City Department of Education (NYC DOE), the Children's Aid Society Community School at Intermediate School 218, and Public School 5 in one of NYC's most disadvantaged neighborhoods, Washington Heights.

Founded on the principles of Dewey and Adams, the Children's Aid Society Community School (CASCS) model became a template for other school community partnerships across NYC and across the nation.

The demand for information about partnerships between community organizations and public schools grew and grew. Different groups wanted to coordinate efforts to help children and their families, and wanted help in structuring and implementing the community school model. Two years after the first CASCS, CAS created the National Center for Community School (NCCS) to provide information about community schools. The NCCS, which has gathered information from community schools across the nation, serves as an advocacy group for the community school movement.

A small group of community school advocates joined forces in 1997 and founded the Coalition for Community Schools ("100 Years of History," n.d.). The Coalition is housed at the Institute for Educational Leadership. More than 170 national, state, and local organizations in education, K-16, belong to it. The Coalition's website (http://www.communityschools.org/aboutschools/about_community_schools_.aspx) contains a wealth of resources for school leaders to use as they endeavor to create community partnerships.

NATIONAL YOUTH SERVICE AND DEVELOPMENT ORGANIZATIONS

National youth service and development programs such as the Girl Scouts, Boy Scouts, 4-H Clubs, the National Alliance for Youth Sports, and the Boys and Girls Clubs of America have a similar philosophy to the community school movement. These organizations believe that learning is best done by doing and offer programs, supported by adult mentors/leaders, to develop skills, character, citizenship, and service to better the lives of youth and their community.

Girl Scouts

The Girl Scouts (GS) is a national and international organization that helps girls develop into leaders. Beyond their famous annual cookie sales, the Girl Scouts proudly claim to offer "the best leadership development experience for girls in the world" (Girl Scouts of the United States of America, 2016–2019b, para 1). Its mission is to make the world a better place by supporting courage, confidence, and character in an all-girl setting. Programs are run by girls, for girls, and strive for every member to find her G.I.R.L. (go-getter, innovator, risk-taker, and leader) (Girl Scouts of the United States of America, 2016–2019c).

The GS Leadership Experience's foundation taps into the areas of science, technology, engineering, and math (STEM), outdoors, life skills, and entrepreneurship. Each girl creates her own adventure, learning by doing. "While she may be exposed to these subjects at school, in other youth programs, or even on her own, at Girl Scouts she'll experience them in a unique way that puts her on a path to a lifetime of leadership, adventure, and success" (Girl Scouts of the United States of America, 2016–2019d, para 7).

Through the GS Leadership program, girls gain a strong sense of self, demonstrate positive values, take on challenges and use setbacks to improve, develop healthy relationships, and find solutions to problems in their community (The Girl Scouts of the United States of America, 2016–2019d). An example of these characteristics in action comes from GS Troop 20269 of the Southern Appalachians (The Girl Scouts of the United States of America, 2016–2019a). A local children's hospital's social media post expressed a need for a sensory tool, The Zipper, which was on exhibit at the local science museum.

The girl scouts went into action. They visited the museum to see The Zipper, and they met the patients who would use The Zipper. Together the troop researched, sketched, and planned the construction of The Zipper. Using funds from their cookie sale, they bought the materials and built The Zipper.

This project supports the components of the GS Leadership Experience (Girl Scouts of the United States of America, 2016–2019a).

It also supports girls in STEM and girls' academic skills (Girl Scouts of the United States of America, 2016–2019a). Similar organizations to consider for school-community partnerships are the Boy Scouts of America and 4-H Clubs.

Boy Scouts of America

Boy Scouts of America (BSA) provides programs to girls and boys from kindergarten to age 20. There are five BSA programs:

- Cub Scouts, grades K-5
- Scouts BSA, ages 11–17
- Venturing, ages 14–20
- Sea Scouting, ages 14–20
- Exploring, ages 10–20.

BSA focuses on experiential learning and service-related character and leadership building. The BSA slogan is to *Do a Good Turn Daily*. The daily goal to do something good for an individual, the community, or the environment without the expectation of a reward or acknowledgement promotes leadership and citizenship (Boy Scouts of America, 2019a).

Sea scouting is a unique program that takes place on national waters: lakes, rivers, and oceans. Activities are scout directed with adults mentoring them. Sea Scouts prepare on land and on the water. For students interested in a future in the military, marine industry, or even recreational boating, Sea Scouting gives them a head start (Boy Scouts of America, 2019b).

4-H Clubs

The four H's of the 4-H organization are *head, heart, hands,* and *health*. 4-H programs operate through a network of cooperative extensions of more than 100 public universities. 4-H programs are open to girls and boys, aged five to eighteen, and fall into three categories: STEM and agriculture, healthy living, and civic engagement. Their program offerings include in-school enrichment, OST activities, summer camps, and clubs. What makes 4-H programs different from others is the university-backed curriculum experiences rather than traditional classroom-type instruction (National 4-H, 1902–2019b).

While 4-H runs programs in urban, suburban, and rural areas, their Rural Youth Development (RYD) grant program is unique. The National 4-H Council partners with more than 100 public universities to address the specific needs of rural youth. The program seeks to empower rural youth and make them partners of their community through OST programs, governance, decision-making, and volunteer development (National 4-H, 1902–2019a).

National Alliance for Youth Sports (NAYS)

The National Alliance for Youth Sports (NAYS) is a partnership network of CBOs that believes participation in sports promotes valuable life skills. NAYS empowers communities and families through education about sports and the donation of sports equipment. This alliance partners with other national CBOs such as local parks and recreation departments, Boys and Girls Clubs, Police Athletic Leagues, YMCAs/YWCAs, and U.S. military installations (National Alliance for Youth Sports, 2019a).

In the area of youth development, the NAYS has three programs: Start Smart; Ready, Set, RUN!; and Hook a Kid on Golf. Each is structured as turnkey program in a stress-free environment that is developmentally appropriate for children (National Alliance for Youth Sports, 2019c).

Start Smart is a parent-child program for young children under seven years old. The goal is to prepare children for sports participation by developing motor skills and building confidence in a fun, safe environment. NAYS provides the curriculum of skill development in eight sports. Usually, the Start Smart programs are run through a local youth service agency (National Alliance for Youth Sports, 2019e).

Ready, Set, RUN! is a twelve-week program designed to prepare youth, ages eight to thirteen years, to run a 5K race. Along with preparing the youth physically and nutritionally, the curriculum includes goal setting, self-esteem, and confidence building. Often the Ready, Set, RUN! program is offered to support a community's existing 5K run. In addition to being easy to follow and set up, the program includes character and community building activities (National Alliance for Youth Sports, 2019d).

Hook a Kid on Golf's goal is to provide youth with accessibility to golf. They want golf to be as available to youth as other sports such as baseball and soccer. The program's curriculum has three developmental levels: tee, green, and challenge. Equipment and instructions are included. The program is designed so that an individual, a youth agency, or a golf course could implement it (National Alliance for Youth Sports, 2019b).

Boys and Girls Clubs of America

The Boys and Girls Clubs attest that participants of their programs are more likely to graduate from high school, be physically active, and volunteer in their community. Their goal is to provide access to all youth and to develop character, citizenship, and healthy habits (Boys & Girls Clubs of America, n.d.a). The Boys and Girls Clubs offer a myriad of programs for youth aged from six to eighteen. The programs fall into six major categories:

- sports and leisure
- health and wellness
- the arts
- education
- character and leadership
- career development.

They are also partners with the NAYS network of organizations (Boys & Girls Clubs of America, n.d.c).

In the education category, the Boys and Girls Clubs' programs support globally competent graduates to achieve their mission of their members graduating from high school. There are ten academic success programs:

- Career Launch
- Computer Pathways
- diplomas2Degrees
- DYI STEM (Do It Yourself Science, Technology, Engineering and Math)
- Junior Staff
- Money Matters
- Power Hour
- Project Learn
- Summer Brain Gain
- Tech Girls Rock.

Each program supports members in their academic endeavors from tutoring to college preparation and admission so members can graduate from high school college-ready and on time (Boys & Girls Clubs of America, n.d.b).

Of interest is the tutoring and homework help program for students ages 6–18, Power Hour: Making Minutes Count. The program provides engaging strategies and activities to enable members to become independent and self-reliant learners.

Meaningful community partnerships can be formed with any of the programs mentioned above. It could mean hosting a girl scout or boy scout troop at your school, co-sponsoring a specific program from the 4-H Clubs or the National Alliance for Youth Sports, or forming a partnership with the Boys and Girls Clubs of America. Positive relationships with these youth service and development organizations contribute to developing your students' potential for well-rounded success.

COMMUNITY-BASED ORGANIZATIONS (CBOs)

National and international service organizations are accustomed to partnering with schools and they often have a wealth of resources and experience. There are also many CBOs at the local level that can provide goods and services to fill the gap between what schools have and what schools need. Students often encounter many issues that impact their learning that are not school related.

These nonacademic barriers—housing and food instability, conflict, aggression, disorganization, and poor peer and community relationships—can be mitigated through partnerships with CBOs (Anderson-Butcher, Stetler, & Midle, 2006).

Partnerships between schools and community organizations can positively affect students, their parents, and teachers. Students learn new talents and skills, become aware of career opportunities and community resources, and make community connections. Parents interact with other parents and the community, become aware of resources and opportunities for their families, and see the community's role in their children's education.

Teachers in the school gain an awareness of the community's assets and resources that can enhance curriculum, become open to collaborating with community members in their classrooms, and become knowledgeable of the potential support community organizations can provide for their students and their families (Epstein, 2010). One partnership option to consider with CBOs is OST activities at the school.

OST partnerships can help narrow the achievement gap, improve students' health and wellness, develop a sense of community and volunteerism, and develop students' leadership and character. There are three domains of OST programs and activities: academic, prevention or social services, and extracurricular (Anderson-Butcher et al., 2006). Table 5.1 lists possible school-community OST partnerships organized by category.

CBOs are valuable community assets for forming partnership with knowledge on *how partnerships are done* in nonacademic and academic areas. Student outcomes can be enhanced through school-community partnerships. Though local CBOs may not have ever partnered with school, ASK! Think WIIFM (What's In It For Me?) and WIIF-Them (What's In It For Them?). Think win-win.

Educational Organizations and Programs

Urban and suburban school districts usually have local educational organizations with which to partner. A local college or university offers a variety of possibilities for partnerships. See chapter 6 for an in-depth discussion. In the

Table 5.1 Possible School-Community OST Partnerships by Categories

Academic	Extracurricular	Prevention/Social Services
Adult literacy and continuing education	Arts and crafts programs	Alcohol, tobacco, and drug prevention and counseling
College/university programs offering credit	Before-school activities	
	Community service clubs	Case management services
Expanded school library hours	Drama activities	Character education
	Family nights and community events	Child care support
Employment counseling	Field trips	Cultural diversity activities
English as a second or new language	Fitness activities	Health and wellness activities
	Intramural sports	
GED/TASC (high school equivalency) exam classes	Mentoring programs	Leadership clubs
	Music	Nursing services
Homework help	Recreational activities	Parent support and education classes
Literacy assistance and enrichment	Service learning activities	
	Summer programs	School transition supports
STEM enrichment	Weekend activities for youth	Smoking cessation
Technology enrichment		Social skills groups
Tutoring	Youth development programs (Girl Scouts, 4-H)	Social work groups
School to work programs		Violence prevention
Students with disabilities support and enrichment		

absence of local institutions of higher education, many CBOs have programs or activities related to education.

Partnerships can be created within a school district with support from educational organizations and community service programs, such as Future Teachers of America (FTA) (Future Teachers of America, n.d.a). High school students can partner with elementary school's classes to be reading buddies and homework tutors, or they can partner with middle-school students as mentors to help with the transition to high school life and demands.

High school students get leadership experiences and satisfy service project requirements of their schools or service and religious organizations. Younger students get academic and emotional support.

FTA considers talented high school students as an untapped resource. They have a training program to support high school students as tutors (Future Teachers of America, n.d.b). FTA also has a telereading program in which their members support struggling elementary and middle-school readers at home using telecommunications technology (Future Teachers of America, n.d.a).

Health Organizations

State and local health departments, hospitals, clinics, foundations, and associations are avenues for community-school partnerships. Partnerships with health organizations can fit into in-school programs and activities as well as the three OST domains (academic, extracurricular, and prevention/social services).

In response to the projected need for health-care professionals in its state, Indiana initiated statewide programs to connect workforce development with education by developing medical magnet schools. When new principal Lauren Franklin came to Crispus Attuck High School in Indianapolis, Indiana, the school was a medical magnet school on paper only with few medical courses. She revamped the program and started the certified nursing assistant (CNA) program. She decided to address head-on the negative connotation that career education is for those students with poor or weak academic skills (McCoy, 2018).

To enter the CNA, prospective health professional high school students must have at least a 3.0 grade point average, a strong record of attendance, pass a background check, and pass a health exam. The students earn high school credit, get paid for working in a medical clinic, and become CNAs. Lauren formed partnerships with the government and a local health agency to give her high school students a head start into the health professions.

Social Service Organizations

Social service organizations are providers of a wide variety of services. They can be public, private, for profit, nonprofit, or governmental. Inherently, they strive to help make communities stronger by supporting equity and opportunity. They are a natural fit for school-community partnerships. Community social service organization partners can facilitate and support schools in such areas as health care, education, career training, policy research, food and housing security, community management, and community safety (Wikipedia, 2019b).

United Way. The United Way is an international service organization with branches throughout the United States and the world. Its mission aligns well with the formation of partnerships. "We create positive and permanent change by forging unlikely partnerships, finding new solutions to old problems and mobilizing the best resources. But we don't do it alone" (United Way, 2019b, para 5). The United Way seeks "the common good in communities across the world" by supporting the "building block for a good quality of life": education, income, and health (United Way, 2019a, para 1).

Since Marc Baiocco became superintendent of Elmsford Union Free School District in Elmsford, New York, he has looked for ways to form partnerships with organizations and individuals in his community to bring resources and funds into his schools. (See more about his skills and abilities as an entrepreneurial leader in chapter 7.)

He sees these partnerships as a win-win for his community partners and his schools. He has two partnerships with United Way. One partnership involves a three-way agreement with Learning Ovations, which is a professional support system that combines technology and professional development to improve K-3 students' literacy rates. Learning Ovations is part of a federally funded program, United2Read, aimed at closing the achievement gap nationwide.

The United Way is funding a large portion of this program so that Marc's primary teachers can receive customized training and support for implementing Learning Ovations' computerized assessment system to help with data-driven instruction. Students take assessments every six weeks. Teachers use this assessment system to determine how to group their students for meaning and coding. These primary teachers are using the data to personalize instruction, which is helping with students' reading gains.

The second partnership with United Way is to stop the Summer Slide. United Way is providing funding for instructors so that his students, grades PK-6, can participate in a summer reading program for six weeks. Additionally, United Way will be helping to host a series of Family Reading and Picnic events over the summer months. As Marc said, he is incredibly appreciative of his partnerships with United Way because of the help that his students are receiving.

Government and Military Agencies

Most governmental and military organizations have an implied and real connection to community, locally and nationally. They are in the business of serving and volunteering for communities. Look into what your local police and fire departments have to offer. They are resources for safety instructions, tutoring, mentoring, internships, and career guidance. Your local chamber of commerce, city council, and other governmental agencies can be the source of revenue, experience, and expertise in a variety of fields.

Schools located near federal public lands and waterways can partner with Hands on the Land (HOL). Sponsored by Partners in Resource Education, HOL is a national network of field classrooms. Its educational programs promote conservation education in natural, historical, and archaeological environments such as national parks, forests, wildlife refuges, and recreation areas. Students and teachers collaborate with federal employees to learn the basics about these environments. The curriculum is designed for students to develop the STEM skills of investigating and evaluating to make environmental decisions (Hands on the Land Network, 2001–2019).

There are many other national service and volunteer organizations that could be tapped for partnerships. Search the National Service website https

://www.nationalservice.gov/serve/search for service and volunteer organizations. Put in your zip code for a list of potential national organizations with which to partner. Table 5.2 provides a list of potential national service and volunteer organizations to consider.

Faith Organizations

Faith organizations, such as churches, synagogues, and mosques, are known for their generosity. Your local faith organizations can provide volunteers in the form of tutors, mentors, and coaches. They also can provide food, school supplies, and physical space. Principal Lou D'Ambrosio of Arthur Middleton Elementary School, Waldorf, Maryland took a page from Cassandra in the opening vignette. He also believes it takes a village, and he hosted a Pastors' Breakfast (D'Ambrosio, 2018).

A bit concerned about blurring the lines between church and state, he charged forward because he wanted to increase community involvement in his school. He tapped the pastors as leaders of their community to support the children and their families. At the first Pastors' Breakfast, he asked for volunteers for his school's Reading Buddies program. He was immediately rewarded when one minister volunteered and then enlisted other congregants to do the same (D'Ambrosio, 2018).

Sororities and Fraternities

The mention of sororities and fraternities might conjure up the vision of unruly college students and *Animal House*. While there is usually a social element to their organizations, many exist for the purpose of philanthropy and character or leadership development. Others are related to a specific profession, ethnicity, culture, or religion (Wikipedia, 2019a). Members of sororities and fraternities who live in your community can become partners with your schools. They can provide materials and supplies and serve as mentors, guest speakers, tutors, and career counselors.

Table 5.2 Potential National Service and Volunteer Organizations

AARP	Kiwanis Club	Unites States
Americorp	Knights of Columbus	Government
Boys and Girls Club	4-H Club	United Way
Boy Scouts	Lions Club	Urban League
Concerned Black Men, Inc.	Minority Student	VISTA
Elks	Achievement Network	VFW
Freemans	Rotary Club	YMCA & YWCA
Girl Scouts	Shriners	
Hands on the Land	Senior Corp	

Delta Sigma Theta Sorority is an example of a service sorority dedicated to scholarship and community service to the Black community. The Suffolk (Virginia) Alumnae Chapter of Delta Sigma Theta Sorority also endorses the African proverb, "It takes a village to raise a child." Each year this sorority fulfills one of its program initiatives, educational development, by organizing a school supply drive for the students of Suffolk Public Schools.

This annual event represents a partnership network as the Alumnae Chapter partners with Suffolk Public Schools and the local Boys and Girls Clubs to identify recipients of the supplies. Members of the local Mid-Atlantic Material Test Laboratory of the Norfolk Naval Shipyard Code # 134 donate the school supplies (Staff Reports, 2018).

Cultural and Recreational Organizations

The list of possible partnerships with cultural and recreational organizations is limitless. Cultural organizations include the areas of music, dance, art, theater, film, and photography as well as organizations related to ethnic cultures (e.g., Italian American Culture Center of New Orleans, Louisiana and Schomburg Center for Research in Black Culture in New York City). Recreational and leisure organizations represent sports, pastimes, and hobbies.

The types of organizations are vast. They could be sport teams, computer clubs, booster clubs, zoos, botanical gardens, woodworking groups, hunting clubs, museums, or libraries. Partnerships with cultural and recreational organizations can help to improve student achievement and develop student character and leadership.

Cultural and recreational organizations also help to combat schools' lack of resources for arts education. School leaders in New Orleans, Louisiana and Dallas, Texas formed partnerships with local arts and culture groups to fill an art gap. KID smART of New Orleans connects local artists with teachers to provide professional development and teacher residencies. Dallas' Big Thought program offers art education partnerships with after-school and summer opportunities.

Two other art organizations, Boston's Art Expansion Initiative and Seattle's Creative Advantage, create art databases and guides, especially to support school leaders in matching schools' art needs to art resources (Bowen & Kisida, 2017).

Individual Community Members

Forming partnerships, formal or informal, with local community members brings the concept of partnerships full circle. They bring the community into the school and the school into the community. The most valuable relationships begin with contact, person to person. Your individual community members are natural resources with a wide variety of skills, knowledge, and expertise. Your local business owners, public servants, parents, grandparents, teachers, senior citizens, and school employees all have something to share that could inform and enhance students' lives.

When you see or meet with members of the community, get to know them. What skill or knowledge do they possess that could enhance the lives of your students? Call upon them to share their wealth of experiences. Share your school's mission, goals, and needs with them. Welcome them into your classrooms and students' lives.

CREATING COMMUNITY PARTNERSHIPS

As Robert Smith (2010) pointed out, schools, especially those serving racially, economically and linguistically diverse populations, need *allies* to support their students morally, socially, politically, and intellectually. Beyond a single partnership with a single school or school district, CBOs can connect to each other and easily create a network of services and programs that not only support the school, but also reach out to the students' families and their community.

Many CBOs' missions are to serve the community, advocate for their cause, and volunteer their time, resources, and expertise. They need entrepreneurial school leaders to partner with them to meet their organizations' goals and missions. They can bring the community into the school. The school in turn can then move out of the school into the community. Match the goals.

- Look into the national youth organizations. Start by studying their websites. What are their missions and goals? Do they fit your school's need? Can they fill the gaps of services and support that you need? What is the cost?
- Seek out health and wellness nonprofits and organizations. What services do your students and families need? Where are the organizations located? How can they help your students? What can your school or district offer them?
- Enlist your local community. Look around your community from the government to individual community members. Which individuals and organizations match your school's needs and goals?

Explore CBOs' initiatives. Match the initiatives with your school's goals. Determine your WIIFMS. Prepare a WIIFT list. Align them. It's win-win!

Consider a Full-Service Community School

Consider the power and potential impact a constellation of wraparound services could do for your school. Consider developing partnerships that fulfill not only your students' academic needs but also their physical and emotional needs. A full-service community school can make a difference in the lives of your students, their families, and the community at large. Full-service community schools can offer:

- Basic needs
- Access to health care
- Literacy readiness
- Quality education
- Extended learning opportunities
- Positive school environment
- Parent involvement
- Opportunities for community service
- Supportive adults
- Integrated services
- Safe communities
- Lifelong learning (Dryfoos & Maguire, 2002).

Do any of the above items that a full-service community school can offer align with what your school needs or wants?

Cassandra, from our opening vignette, has many of the above elements in place and is on the path to becoming a full-service community school. She attributes the formation of many of her partnerships and financial support for them to her district's Coordinator of Grants and Partnership Development, Marcia Oglesby. Cassandra feels "blessed" to have her as a member of her "village." A true entrepreneurial leader, Cassandra connected with Marcia to add to her constellation of individuals, organizations, and agencies that would help to improve her school.

Together, Marcia and Cassandra have secured grants to support literacy, STEM, and social-emotional professional development from their governor's office, the DART Foundation, Handson Atlanta, and the DeKalb County Public Library. They have built in partnership sustainability so that organizations will contribute long-term to Cassandra's community school framework.

LEADERSHIP TO ORGANIZE AND CREATE A COMMUNITY SCHOOL

A review of the Coalition for Community School's website is a valuable place to start when thinking about creating a community school or exploring how to go about developing CBOs as partners. There are National Community School Standards; guidelines for how to start a community school. These guidelines help with developing a vision and strategic plan, building a leadership team, assessing needs and capacity, sharing space and facilities, financing, and conducting research and evaluation.

There also are publications, advocacy documents, videos, and models of community schools across the nation on this website (Coalition for Community Schools at the Institute for Educational Leadership, 2019a).

We are in a data-driven climate. To make a case for creating a community school, entrepreneurial school leaders need to provide data to convince policy makers and other stakeholders that community schools work. Convincing and useful data include attendance challenges, dropout rates, graduation rates, and declining student achievement. The Coalition for Community Schools has an Evaluation Tool Kit that can be used to gather, analyze, and synthesize data.

Additionally, it provides samples of completed evaluations, the sequence of steps to take, and a list of data collection instruments to use. (See Martin J. Blanks, Community Schools Evaluation Toolkit at www.communityschools.org and www.iel.org).

Take a look at the tab labeled *Your Leadership Role* on the Coalition for Community Schools' website. Resources for all levels of leadership are found there. Under the Principal level, the resource categories are reports and articles, cases, tools, and video. Under the Cases tab is Glencliff High School of Nashville, Tennessee as an example of a successful community school and winner of the *2011 Community Schools for Excellence Award.*

Glencliff was experiencing high levels of gang activity and incidences of violence. The school revised its school vision, completed a needs assessment, embraced the community school model, and began filling in the gaps with community partnerships.

By transforming the high school to a community school, forging more than seventy community and business partnerships, and making Glencliff a community hub, their graduation rates and student performance increased significantly. When surveyed, 81 percent of Glencliff's students felt more connected to the community, particularly with the adults in their community, and 70 percent reported their school climate had improved as a result of being a community school (Institute for Educational Leadership, 2011). Creating a full-service community school does not happen all at once.

You need to have a vision, goals, a step-by-step plan, a collaborative spirit, and perseverance in order to achieve a functional full-service community school. A bit of luck helps, too!

LEADERSHIP TO FORM COMMUNITY PARTNERSHIPS

Effective leadership impacts student achievement. Effective leaders have high expectations for students and faculty, provide multiple support systems, are resourceful and

> utilize a variety of leadership practices to develop formal and informal linkages with multiple community sources to help accomplish their mission. Valuable school-community linkages are based on the collaboration and active engagement of parent and constituencies from throughout the school and the community. (Masumotos & Brown-Welty, 2009, p. 15)

Be intentional and clear with your goals as you seek local and national organizations to be your partners. Consider potential conflicts of interests with your goals. Use data to initiate and support your partnerships. Take tender care of your partnerships and their relationships.

Chapter 6

Partnerships with Colleges and Universities

Scott Mastroianni served as principal of The Flory Academy of Sciences and Technology, a Title I public Transitional K-5 STEM Magnet school in Moorpark, California from 2014 to 2018. When he became principal at Flory, he inherited a typical Professional Development School (PDS) with California Lutheran University. Each year Flory would welcome teacher candidates from California Lutheran University who were placed with mentor teachers for an entire school year.

Having a strong partnership allowed for two-way support between Flory and the university. This support included providing a dedicated classroom for the university to hold classes, university supervisors regularly coming on campus to supervise teacher candidates, and Flory staff occasionally serving as adjunct faculty in the credential program. Additionally, both organizations would share in professional learning opportunities provided by the district or the university.

Scott came to Flory with strong beliefs about mentorship and coaching. He believed that the PDS could do more to support teacher candidates in his building. He follows Steve Farber's (2009) leadership model of "greater than yourself" and believes that experiences shape beliefs. He decided that, as a principal, he would become very involved with each candidate to help them develop into teachers, grow their resumes, and provide rich and relevant experiences to help prepare them for a future in education. With his hands-on leadership style, he invested in each candidate, made himself available to them, and some years held monthly luncheons with anywhere from six to ten teacher candidates in order to celebrate accomplishments, discuss situations and experiences, and exchange ideas.

Scott wanted them to have a safe space to discuss ways to handle situations with parents and cooperating teachers. He also wanted them to feel included in the life of the school so he made sure to include them on all emails, parent conferences, IEP meetings, etc. In essence, they were considered as equal and valuable members of the staff. He considers the PDS candidate experience as a yearlong interview that enables candidates to make connections with and have a significant impact on students and families. The yearlong experience allows candidates to get a true sense of an entire year; from the excitement of school opening, the ups and downs throughout the school year, to the final week of school.

His mentor teachers had to be invested in the co-teaching model, have a coaching mindset, and have an open mind to learning and growing themselves. They also had to participate in the "match day" process in which Flory and California Lutheran University established to successfully pair the mentor teachers with teacher candidates. He found that when the teacher candidate-mentor teacher pairs were a natural fit for each other, there were positive outcomes. Student teachers developed into well-prepared, new teachers who were readily employable for the district and veteran teachers developed professionally by learning about new theories, teaching styles, and technology.

He admits he had an ulterior motive for expanding the role of his PDS in teacher preparation. If teacher candidates were well prepared, they provided his district with a cadre of future teachers to hire. However, more importantly, he could help shape and mold candidates that were going to help improve public education for all kids.

Scott is now principal of E. P. Foster STEM Academy in Ventura, California. His new mission is to transform Foster into a PDS. His new school receives requests from several college/universities to take student teachers at E. P. Foster, but he wants to have a formal Memorandum of Understanding (MOU) with a university that enables him to replicate the program that he had with California Lutheran University. He is taking small steps by having conversations with university representatives who are interested in placing teacher candidates at his school for the full year.

His advice to other educational leaders who are seeking to create a school-college/university partnership is to "Embrace it and invest in it because the return on investment is huge. Look beyond the notion of the idea of free labor. Appreciate the positive impact it has on students and your school community. Share resources and be a champion of this powerful opportunity so that you can see it as a win-win-win"!

POSSIBLE PARTNERSHIPS WITH COLLEGES AND UNIVERSITIES

In the early history of school-college/university partnerships, colleges and universities were often the initiators of partnership with K-12 schools. They needed schools to serve as sites for research and future teachers' fieldwork (Walsh & Backe, 2013). The partnerships tended to be one-sided.

In the late 1980s, Sirotnik (1991) and his colleague John Goodlad described their notion of school-university partnerships as "a deviant idea and it is an idea whose time has come" (p. 15). Key to their *deviant idea* of partnership was collaboration to solve problems in a manner that would be mutually rewarding. A response to the more recent school reforms to seek equity in K-12 students' educational experiences is a more balanced school-college/university partnership (Walsh & Backe, 2013). All parties involved get and give something that the other needs or wants. What was a deviant idea then is commonplace now for successful school-university partnerships; in other words, WIIFM and WIIFT (What's In It For Me? What's In It For Them?); win-win.

There are multiple variations of school-college/university partnerships. The variation ranges from a partnership between an individual college/university faculty member and an individual K-12 school faculty member to a statewide required PDS system between the state university's schools of education and all of the state's public schools (e.g., Georgia and Maryland). They can be short-term and project oriented or long-term and transformational.

TYPES OF PARTNERSHIPS

Epstein (1995) developed a framework of partnership types between schools, communities, and families: parenting, communication, volunteering, learning at home, decision-making, and collaboration with the community. Her Six Major Types of Partnerships Framework is an applicable model for school-college/university partnership development.

For example, a school seeks a college/university partnership to improve student achievement. The goals of the partnership are communicated to all stakeholders. All the stakeholders take part in the decision-making on how to reach the goals. The goal and resources needed to reach the goal are communicated to the community. The college/university provides resources and training to guide parents in collaborating to reach the goals. The partnership supports the goals through school, university, and community volunteers. The college/university teaches parents strategies they can use at home to help close the achievement gap.

School-college/university partnerships generally link college and university functions with the domains of learning. College/university's functions are teaching, research, and service. The domains are educational leadership, curriculum and instruction, and student support (Walsh & Backe, 2013). Figure 6.1 displays these components. Generally, three types of college/

university involvement in the school-college/university partnerships range from general to more specific in focus: (1) school-college/university, (2) school-college/university school of education, and (3) professional development school-college/university. The type of the partnership will depend on which is best to meet the mutual goals of the school and its college/university partners.

Type 1: School-College/University Partnerships

Colleges and universities depend on schools. They are interdependent and connected. They have a shared mission to educate. School curricula are designed to prepare students for college. Colleges and universities need high school graduates who want to continue their education (Shive, 1984). Society needs both to be successful.

One of the main reasons schools want to partner with a college or university is to boost or improve student achievement (Wepner et al., 2012). One way to do so is to provide professional development and college/university level courses to faculty and students. Partner college and university

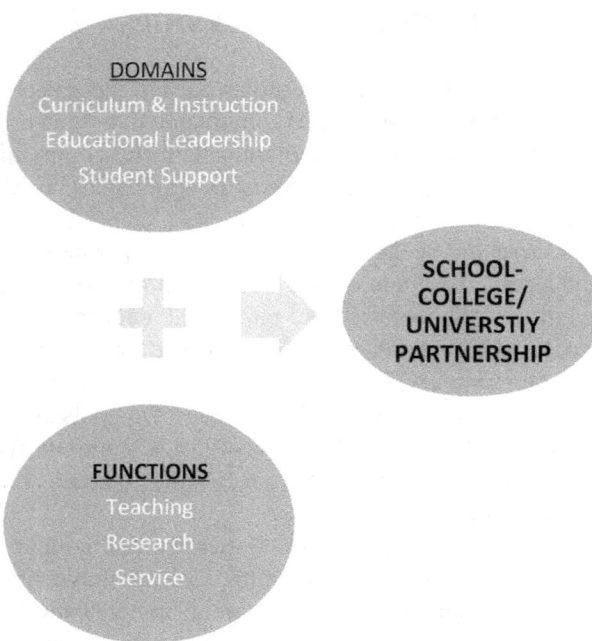

Figure 6.1   College/University Components of School Partnerships.

professors teach their areas of expertise to the school's faculty so that they keep up-to-date with curriculum content, technology, and licensure mandates.

Professional development can be delivered to teachers at their school or on a college/university campus through lectures, workshops, seminars, or small-group sessions. It also can be provided through co-teaching and modeling instruction in the teachers' classroom or performing action research. Providing professional development to teachers can increase their knowledge base in certain subjects (e.g., geography or computer science) and, in turn, enhance their students' learning and academic achievement.

Students' academic opportunities can be enhanced by offering college level courses to high school students. This can be accomplished by matching a desired content to be taught with a college/university professor in that field. Generally, such courses are taught on-site at the high school or in a virtual format. High school graduates can enter college as freshmen with college credit.

Students' skills can be sharpened in areas other than traditional academics. Max Dehne, assistant professor at State University of New York (SUNY) at Delhi partnered with the local elementary school to form the after-school club, *Design & Build*. College architecture students worked as teaching assistants with sixth-graders to design, build, and install a playground. The sixth-graders learned architecture, science, and carpentry. This project extended the partnership to community members. The local hospital, Rotary Club, and Complete Streets provided assistance (Karikehalli, 2019).

Teachers can also benefit from partnerships that offer college and university graduate courses on-site at their schools or in the community. School leaders are often seeking teachers with multiple certifications or licenses. Many states require that their teachers stay current in their field in order to maintain licensure which requires courses outside of the field of education. Additionally, the completion of college/university courses can be considered in their application for an increase in salary.

When New York State passed new requirements to improve the academic outcomes for English learners (ELs), a partner school contacted Manhattanville College to help already certified teachers meet the new regulations. Many teachers were interested in not only meeting the new requirements, but also obtaining certification in teaching ELs.

To become a certified teacher of ELs, teachers need twelve credits of a world language. Many mid-career teachers had taken a world language as undergraduates, but most did not have the required twelve credits. The majority had earned six to eight credits of a world language. They did not feel confident, after several years of not studying a world language, to continue studying the language at the mid- and upper-levels. The partnership solution between the school and the college's department of world languages was to develop a cohort of interested teachers and offer six credits of a new language—American Sign Language.

Type 2: School-College/University School of Education Partnerships

Schools and college/university schools of education share many common goals. Both are interested in curriculum development/improvement, leadership development, articulation between college/university and school curriculum and courses, professional development, research in educational theory and practice, and qualified and employable teachers (Shive, 1984). Schools of education are professional units of their colleges and universities. They need "the education of educators . . . close to the heart of their mission" and "solid connections to the field" (Sirotnik, 1991, p. 20). School-college/university partnerships create a pipeline of future teachers that school administrators can get to know while student teaching in their schools and provide potential research opportunities for professors. College/university administrators and faculty who see school faculty in action can employ them as adjunct instructors.

A school partnership with a college/university School of Education can offer the same resources and services as those of school-college/university partnerships. A school partnership with a School of Education has a specific focus on teacher and leader preparation. Often, a school or school system calls on a School of Education for guidance in the areas of curriculum, instruction, and/or assessment through graduate courses, teacher professional development, and/or parent engagement.

The School of Education provides support in the areas of need and can use the partnership school as a site for research for college/university faculty, teacher and leader candidate placements, field-based preparation and practice for teacher and leader candidates, and volunteerism of college/university faculty in the community. Schools become a living laboratory to apply educational theory to practice.

The UCLA Center X-LAUSD Partnership was developed to support content literacy instruction, standards-based instruction, and instructional leadership for Los Angeles Unified School District (LAUSD) Local District 1's high schools. The partnership included LAUSD school leaders, teachers, and parent leaders. The University of California Los Angeles (UCLA) provided support from teacher educators, professional developers, and professors. The goal was to provide content-based literacy professional development to improve high schoolers' literacy achievement (MacDonald & Dorr, 2005).

Each high school content area department (English, mathematics, social studies, and science) received professional development through literacy coaches in their classrooms. University content coaches met monthly with teachers outside their classrooms, but in their schools during school hours to develop curriculum with literacy strategies in content areas. This was accomplished by hiring substitute teachers. Each content area department at each high school designated a *cadre leader* to meet monthly with the university coaches. The cadre leaders ensured ongoing communication and feedback on challenges and successes of the partnership (MacDonald & Dorr, 2005). This partnership extended beyond the university's School of Education to include professors for the areas of social studies, English, mathematics, and science.

In an age of data-driven decision-making, Portland Public Schools District used their partnership with the University of Portland's School of Education to gather real-time research data to conduct a program evaluation. Their school district-university partnership studied the longitudinal effect of their early kindergarten transition program. The results from the study gave the school district current data to decide whether to continue, maintain, or expand the transitional kindergarten program. The project indirectly set up improved systems for the school district's data collection and analyses. The university professors conducted research and published their findings (Tarasawa, Ralson, & Waggoner, 2016), which influenced university course content and field-based practices. The partnership was mutually beneficial.

Type 3: Professional Development Schools-College/University Partnerships

PDSs are formalized partnerships between a school or school district and a college/university school of education. The PDS model is similar to the medical school model in which teaching, learning, and mentoring are done on-site, in context, with real situations.

Unlike Type 2 partnerships, to be considered a PDS requires that all nine components of the National Association for Professional Development Schools (NAPDS) *Nine Essentials* are in place. The *Nine Essentials* were developed specifically to distinguish PDSs from other types of school-college/university partnerships (National Association for Professional Development Schools, 2008, 2019).

The nine required essentials of a PDS are:

1. A comprehensive mission that is broader in its outreach and scope than the mission of any partner and that furthers the education profession and its responsibility to advance equity within schools and, by potential extension, the broader community
2. A school–university culture committed to the preparation of future educators that embraces their active engagement in the school community

3. Ongoing and reciprocal professional development for all participants guided by need
4. A shared commitment to innovative and reflective practice by all participants
5. Engagement in and public sharing of the results of deliberate investigations of practice by respective participants
6. An articulation agreement developed by the respective participants delineating the roles and responsibilities of all involved
7. A structure that allows all participants a forum for ongoing governance, reflection, and collaboration
8. Work by college/university faculty and P-12 faculty in formal roles across institutional settings
9. Dedicated and shared resources and formal rewards and recognition structures (National Association for Professional Development Schools, 2019, n.p.).

The Nine Essentials embrace the *deviant* notion of mutual benefits through equality in leadership and responsibilities. Scott Mastrioianni clearly focused on addressing many of these nine essentials when he revamped the student teaching component of Flory's PDS.

Charlotte-Mecklenburg (North Carolina) PDS with University of North Carolina at Charlotte began The Teacher Education Institute (TEI) as a collaborative project to investigate coaching as a means to support teacher candidates. They were aware of the research on the effects of instructional coaching on the practicing teacher. TEI sought to further the research by applying an instructional coaching model to teacher candidates (Polly, Diegmann, Kennedy, Brigman, & Luce, 2019).

The TEI ran a four-day summer institute to train college faculty, student teaching supervisors, and clinical faculty in three *high leverage practice* areas: managing group work, getting and interpreting student responses, and leading group discussions. In the fall, trained faculty coached student teachers using the practices. The action research included four individual perspectives: student teacher, elementary school faculty, university student teacher supervisor, and methods professor.

As a result of the action research, all parties arrived at the same understanding of effective teaching. Student teachers felt better prepared to teach and adjust lessons. The elementary teachers became more intentional in lesson planning. University faculty became more proactive in giving immediate feedback to help student teachers with their challenges. The methods professor was more reflective and more supportive to teacher candidates before, during, and after the observed lesson. This one collaborative research project specifically addressed NAPDS essentials listed above of broadening outreach

(#1) and having a shared commitment to innovative and reflective practice (#4) (Polly et al., 2019).

Leadership. In practice, a PDS generally has an organized leadership structure with cross-institution members in the forms of a PDS liaison and a PDS leadership team. A PDS sets the stage for a long-term reciprocal partnership that is focused on innovation and reform.

PDS Liaisons. The PDS liaison is usually a School of Education faculty assigned to one or more PDSs to represent the college/university. He or she spends anywhere from one to five days on-site at the school. The liaison is the conduit between the PDS and the college/university. He or she is the person on the ground and in the field who is supporting and sustaining the PDS relationship. Specific roles and responsibilities vary among PDS partnerships. The liaison, who is crucial to the success of a PDS, needs to have strong leadership and communication skills.

Typically, the primary role of the PDS liaison is to supervise and mentor student teachers/interns who are student teaching or completing fieldwork at the PDS. Other activities include providing professional development for teachers and staff, offering college courses on-site, organizing school events for students and their parents, being a member of school committees, and collaborating in research (Ferrara & Gómez, 2014; Hovda, 1999; Wepner et al., 2012).

PDS Leadership Team. College/university and school faculty govern the day-to-day operations of a PDS through a PDS leadership team. The teams are usually composed of the school principal, teacher representatives, and the PDS liaison or site-based college/university representative. Some PDSs include student/intern teachers, parents, and school staff on their leadership team. These individuals help to broaden the perspectives and can increase commitment to the partnership. Leadership teams promote recognition and advocacy for the PDS. The leadership team meets regularly to determine policies, coordinate activities, and resolve conflicts and issues related to the PDS partnership (Castle, Arenda, & Rockwood, 2008).

PROMISES AND CHALLENGES

School partnerships with a college/university can be a path to school reform. These partnerships invigorate teachers and professors. They encourage taking risks and testing out innovations, strategies, curriculum, and methods. They offer a fertile environment for research by professors and teachers. They foster reflection and assessment (Eargle, 2013). School-college/university partnerships provide promise for all stakeholders associated with the school and the college or university when Sirotnik and Goodlad's deviant concept of mutual benefits is employed.

Promises

Successful partnership characteristics include strong communication and trust among partners, a shared vision, structures for rewarding and compensating participants, and a system of accountability (Gómez, Wepner, & Quatroche, 2017, 2019; Hovda, 1999; Shive, 1984). The most important element of a successful school-college/university partnership is communication. Clear and constant communication facilitates and sustains the key elements of a partnership (Gómez et al., 2017, 2019; MacDonald & Dorr, 2005; Wepner et al., 2012).

Communication. Communication is at the heart of developing and maintains a thriving partnership. It is critical to keep an open line of communication across all levels of the partnership. Include and listen to all stakeholders, not just the policy makers. This can be accomplished by scheduling regular check-ins about what is happening, what is working, and what might not be working. Give time and space for discussions. Scott from the opening vignette is a good example of fostering communication with his student teachers, mentor teachers, and college/university partners.

Explore the best type of communication for the partnership and its members. Together decide which means of communication will work best: face-to-face, phone, conference call, email, text, chat, or Skype. A nonresponse to a message or communication breaks down trust in the commitment to the partnership. Through open communication trust can develop.

Trust. Trust is developed through honesty, action, and example. Dispel the idea that college/university faculty focus on theory and school teachers focus on practical reality. Collaboration demonstrates a commitment to the partnership to develop common ground and common purpose (Sirotnik, 1991). Working together for the common good instills trust as well as respect. Trust among the partners helps eliminate conflicts and facilitates resolutions when conflicts do arise (Walsh & Backe, 2013).

Shared Vision. As a leader you know what your vision is and how it might be accomplished. Your vision needs to be clearly communicated to all stakeholders, from the individual college/university partners to your faculty, to your students, to your families, and to your community. Align your vision with the college/university. Reach consensus on the partnership's vision and goals early in the partnership's development. Consider the context of the work—historically, politically, and socially (Walsh & Backe, 2013). When you co-construct your vision with your college/university partner, include a means for accountability for reaching your mutual goals (MacDonald & Dorr, 2005).

Compensation and Recognition. Members of successful partnerships feel valued, which contributes to ownership and support for the partnership

(Shive, 1984). Appreciation can be shown through compensation and/or recognition. College/university faculty can be compensated for their partnership work in the form of course/time releases and stipends, and as service and valued research to the college/university.

Schools can recognize college/university faculty through resources, visibility, and public acknowledgment. Ways to acknowledge partnership work are press releases, announcements, recognition awards, inclusion in activities and meetings, and invitations to speak and present about the partnership in school, college/university, and community environments. Simple, but appreciated rewards can be access to the school email system, inclusion on the listserv and mailing list to receive school bulletins and reports, inclusion on a list as a member of the school community, and invitations to school social events. One PDS liaison reported she felt rewarded when she was given photocopying privileges and a mailbox at her PDS (Hovda, 1999).

School faculty can be compensated and recognized in many of the same ways. Partnership work can be considered a component of the annual performance review. Release time to participate in partnership and college/university events, teach college courses, research and coauthor action research, earn college/university tuition discounts, and credit toward salary increases are examples of ways to recognize school faculty.

System of Accountability. An assessment system helps to determine the health of a school-college/university partnership. Assessments should include a documentation system of formative and summative assessments that include qualitative and quantitative measures (MacDonald & Dorr, 2005) from all stakeholders. Possible assessment tools for accountability include self-studies, questionnaires, focus groups, surveys, checklists, action research, and student achievement data.

Progress should be assessed on a regular basis, checking in with stakeholders about fidelity to the vision and attainment of goals. If yours is a PDS, continually assess your alignment to the *Nine Essentials* (National Association for Professional Development Schools, 2019), the *Standards for Professional Development Schools* (National Council for Accreditation of Teacher Education, 2001a), and the *Handbook for Assessment of Professional Development Schools* (National Council for Accreditation of Teacher Education, 2001b) (Breault, 2014; Trachtman, 2007). Progress monitoring results and outcomes should be documented and shared with all stakeholders.

Challenges

In the life of a partnership, there are stumbles, trips, and falls. Even long-term partnerships face challenges, particularly those that are complacent. Without the elements above—communication, trust, shared vision, and accountability—a partnership is in danger. Partnerships need an infrastructure to assure its continued success (American Association of Colleges for Teacher Education, 2018). Fidelity, or faithfulness to the key elements of the partnership, can help a relationship overcome obstacles and prevent insurmountable roadblocks.

Strier (2011) characterizes the life of a partnership as a relationship of collaboration and conflict. Unequal division of power is the primary reason for partnership failure (Gray, 2004; Strier, 2011, 2014). The deviant factor of mutuality should be kept in mind.

A working partnership has a constant flow of conflict and collaboration. Seemingly paradoxical, conflict and collaboration are interrelated (Strier, 2014). To negotiate tension and conflict, the entrepreneurial leader can consider three paradoxical types of tension: belonging, informing, and organizing. A belonging paradox refers to relational elements with complementary identities that are clashing. A performing paradox occurs when roles conflict but there is cooperation. An organizational paradox refers to "divergent and convergent organizational sub-cultures" (Strier, 2014, p. 162). To deal with these paradoxes, leaders of school-college/university partnerships need to have *organizational ambidexterity* (Duncan, 1976).

When confronted with a belonging paradox, leaders of partnerships stress the elements of cohesiveness while recognizing power inequalities. If there are performing inequalities, leaders focus on improving internal relations and organizational effectiveness. When there is an organizational paradox of a top-down and bottom-up structure, leaders work toward ameliorating this conflict by nurturing the bottom up while supporting top down (Strier, 2014). Such responses to the three types of paradoxes can also build trust. Identifying the type of conflicts and tensions can be a leadership tool to create collaboration and compromise within the partnership. Common sources of conflict can be anticipated, identified by type, and therefore avoided.

Cultural Clashes. Schools and colleges/universities operate differently and have different work environments. There are differences in work schedules, annual vacation times, roles, responsibilities, goals, and expectations. Help your stakeholders to understand these cultural differences. Communicate orally and in writing about the similarities and differences in the institutions involved with the partnership. Co-construct details related to expectations, roles, and responsibilities that account for these differences and avoid power plays (Walsh & Backe, 2013). Keep your administrative staff in the loop. They are a knowledgeable source of information about the processes, procedures, and point people involved with your partnership at your school.

Expectations. If roles and responsibilities in a partnership are not clearly defined and communicated, assumptions are made and expectations are not met. Expectations between partners at all levels need to be in sync. If the partnership is to be a collaboration, the leaders must communicate expectations clearly and demonstrate through modeling ways in which they are fulfilling their responsibilities (Ledoux & McHenry, 2008).

A university professor comes into a school to provide professional development in technology. He arrives expecting to work with a small group of teachers who are supposed to have a laptop with a particular software. The school administrator gets substitutes for the teachers who are participating and clears the lunchroom so they can all meet at once. A group of twenty-five teachers arrives without laptops. The school has only a handful of laptops without the software. Expectations and responsibilities for the professional development were not communicated or worked out. No one's expectations are met.

Clarity of Roles and Responsibilities. Designating a point person/liaison from each institution facilitates communication, builds trust, and minimizes mismatched expectations. Create a clear description of who does what, with whom, when, and for how long. Leaders should be able to answer the following questions when bringing college/university faculty into a school for a collaborative event:

- Who will be involved in the event?
- What does your school need to do to prepare for the event?
- Where is the event being held? When? For how long?
- Who is the point person responsible for the details of the event?
- How will you communicate with the point person to ensure that plans are in place for the event?
- What resources and information do the college/university faculty member need?
- What preparation and information do the school faculty need?
- In what ways will you assess the value of the event?

As with collaborative events, it is critically important to determine roles and responsibilities when placing a student/intern teacher in your school. The following questions should be answered before making such a commitment for your school:

- Whose responsibility is it to place a student/intern teacher in a classroom?
- What are the school's requirements for placing a student/intern teacher?
- What are the college/university's requirements for placing a student/intern teacher?

- What are the requirements to be a student/intern teacher?
- What are the requirements to be a cooperating/mentor teacher?
- How are the cooperating/mentor and student/intern matched?
- What are the roles and responsibilities of the
  - school leader/administrator?
  - college/university leader/administrator?
  - cooperating/mentor teacher?
  - student/intern teacher?
  - college/university member who supervises the student/intern teacher?
- How is communication facilitated between the cooperating/mentor and the college/university member who supervises the student/intern teacher?
- What is the compensation, if any, for cooperating/mentor who supervises the student/intern teacher?

Time/Schedule. Be mindful of the time that is needed to develop and oversee a school-college/university partnership. Organizing, supporting, and leading a partnership takes time. Partnerships are complex processes that require entrepreneurial leaders to be visionary, resourceful, committed to the concept, communicative, and flexible (Russell & Flynn, 2000). Leaders need to collaborative, visible, and supportive of the partnership's mission and goals (Gómez et al., 2017, 2019; Hovda, 1999; Sirotnik, 1991).

Consider the time constraints and realities for your faculty and staff. Teachers must follow a school's schedule. Teachers have assigned times and places of where to teach and what to teach. College/university professors have more flexibility in how to structure their time and daily schedule. Professors generally teach three to four classes per week. Teachers generally teach all day with a lunch and preparation period per day. Any meetings or events that are scheduled should be considerate of teachers' busy schedules.

Change in Leadership. Leadership changes from either the college/university or the school can affect the school-college/university partnership (Walsh & Backe, 2013). A school leader who is new to a school or school district may have a different vision for the school than his or her predecessor. The new leader needs to review and evaluate the value of an existing school-college/university partnership in relation to his or her vision for the school.

If you are a new leader for your school or district, you could discover that the former leader may have taken his or her partnership and connections with him or her. You might need to renegotiate the terms and conditions of any of the partnerships that existed previously. Review the questions in Table 6.1 to determine whether the partnership is viable and aligned with your school's mission and goals (Hatch, 2009).

Table 6.1 WIIFM (What's In It for Me) and WIIFT (What's In It For Them) Questions

Questions	Responses
Why should we create a school-college/university partnership? • What are the benefits? • What are the risks? • What can be gained from the partnership? • What is the partner's motivation to form the partnership? Does the partnership align with our mission and goals? What will be the intended length of time for the partnership? What are the financial obligations? Do we have the capacity to support a partnership? What will be the impact on our school's faculty, students, parents, and caregivers? • Will the partnership support student learning and success? (American Association of State Colleges and Universities, n. d., p. 18). What will be the impact on university/college faculty, students, and staff? • Will the partnership enhance teaching, learning, and scholarship? (American Association of State Colleges and Universities, n.d.). Will the partnership need physical space? • Where? • Does the space exist? What is the impact on the school community? • On the college/university community? Is there any potential conflict or overlap with any existing partnerships? Is there any possible backlash for forming or not forming the school-college/university partnership? • From administration? • Faculty? • Students? • Parents? • Caregivers? • Community? What would a successful school-university partnership look like? How would success be measured? Is the partnership sustainable? Is the partnership a win-win?	

CREATE PATHWAYS FOR FORMING PARTNERSHIPS WITH COLLEGES AND UNIVERSITIES

Before forming a partnership with a college or university, do your research. Why do you want a partnership? What are your goals and needs? Explore local colleges and universities' websites. What do they have to offer you? Do their offerings match your goals and needs? No institutions of higher education in your area? Do not dismay. A virtual partnership might work, especially if the college/university offers online programs that attract faculty and students in your area. Think outside of the traditional notion of school-college/university partnerships. Use the following guidelines to determine the viability of a school-college/university partnership:

- Reach out to local and regional colleges and universities by contacting different administrative offices and academic departments in education, the arts and sciences, and other professional schools such as engineering and the health sciences. Reach out also to other administrative offices focused on community outreach and alumni outreach.
- Investigate the college/university's history of working with K-12 schools. Begin with the college/university's school or department of education if they have one. What is its partnership experience? Do partnerships already exist with schools similar to yours? If so, what types of partnerships? What evidence of effectiveness exists?
- Determine your school or district's capacity for working with colleges and universities. Do you have leadership capacity, either with you or others? In other words, do you or a point person have the time to plan, develop, and sustain a partnership? Do your faculty have the dispositions to support a partnership? Do you have the physical space? Do you have the resources and financial capacity?
- Determine whether you want to pursue a partnership with one particular department of a college/university, a school or education, or form a PDS. Decide if you are interested in a short- or long-term partnership. In other words, are you looking for a one-time relationship to meet a particular need or goal, or are you interested in forming a long-term relationship that will benefit your school in general?
- Evaluate the financial risks and benefits related to creating a school-college/university partnership. Explore ways to compensate teachers with resources rather than monetary compensation. Look into grants and community support to fulfill the financial obligations of a partnership.
- Examine your stakeholders' potential commitment to a partnership. For example, are your teachers willing to welcome college students and faculty into their rooms to observe or provide professional development? Successful school-college/university partnerships achieve their vision and goals when many or most stakeholders are committed to participating in and supporting the partnership.
- Once you have determined that you have the interest and wherewithal to pursue a partnership, approach a college/university with a list of WIIFT. Sell them on the benefits they will receive through a partnership with you and your school or district.

- Consider a PDS. The PDS partnership model gives schools a liaison who comes to know the school, its faculty, and its community. A liaison is a resource who can deal with real issues and consequences in real time (Hovda, 1999). The school-liaison relationship is solid, intense, and personal. PDS partnerships usually require a long-term commitment so that multiple initiatives can be pursued on behalf of teachers, students, and teacher candidates. The NAPDS website has valuable resources for developing a PDS partnership (see https://napds.org/).

School-college/university partnerships are as unique as the issues they tackle and the environments in which they exist. No two are alike. Entrepreneurial school leaders understand naturally that they need to evaluate their WIIFMs and the college/university's WIIFTs to formulate persuasive arguments for the value of such partnerships. Such leaders know to use both lens—their own and the potential college/university leader's—to develop cogent reasons for motivating their own stakeholders and their contacts at the college/university to enter into a partnership that will be mutually beneficial to both communities.

Chapter 7

Sustaining Partnerships

- *Joe Corcoran, principal of Harriet Gifford Elementary School in Elgin, Illinois, had a partnership with a local bookstore. The children would take walking field trips to the store and while there participate in interactive literature activities. The bookstore arranged with the school many different events. There was "Kids Love a Mystery Night" that had the high school's drama club act out short mini mysteries for the elementary students who had an interactive role. There also was a display of Young Authors stories that included the elementary children's books; a private screening and discussion of a movie at the local movie theater; and a drama event for Black History Month.*

  This came about because the bookstore owner wanted to reconnect to his own children's alma mater and a teacher wanted to pursue this partnership as part of her master's degree coursework (Education World, 1996–2019). Unfortunately, the bookstore closed about three years ago and the partnership dissolved when it closed. As Joe said, "It was a good run while it lasted. Our kids really benefitted from a neighborhood bookstore where they could pop into" (Personal Communication, May 4, 2018).
- *An assistant principal of a middle school in Cincinnati, Ohio shared how she was able to work with small and large businesses in her region to provide many different opportunities for her school. She received funds for students' transportation to theater performances, students' participation in mock trials, copying and printing, the setup of student banks within the school, tutoring students in math, providing food for meetings, and students' participation in after-school clubs. The school closed to allow for other schools in the district to be renovated or rebuilt. Any of the partnerships that had been created were dissolved.*

- *A principal of an elementary suburban school in New York had a partnership with a nonprofit organization to train his primary teachers to use a specialized technique to teach beginning reading. The teachers had volunteered to participate. Pre-post testing showed impressive gains for the children. When this principal left, and a new one was hired, she was not excited by this technique.*

  Even though most of the funding for the training came from the nonprofit organization, she nevertheless did not want to impose this training on her other teachers. She dissolved the partnership within six months of her tenure as principal. The trained teachers ended up having conflicts with the untrained teachers because they were using different techniques to teach beginning reading.

The dissolution of the partnerships described above occurred for different reasons: the closing of a local business, the closing of a school, and the change in administrative leadership. While the first two reasons were beyond the principals' control, the third reason could have been managed during the leadership transition.

UNDERSTANDING SUSTAINABILITY

The ability to sustain a partnership depends on its workability within the context of the school's structure and culture. It means that educational leaders have developed what matters *and* are preserving what matters to the partnership and their school's needs. Educational leaders interested in sustainability engage with partners who share similar values. Together, they continuously learn about the partnership so that they can identify aspects that should be maintained and areas that require new directions. They are imagining ways for the partnership to have long-term capacity (Yendol-Hoppey, Hoppey, & Price, 2011).

This long-term capacity requires support at all levels within one's own institution and the partner institution(s), constant monitoring of partnership activities and initiatives, and the execution of effective communication mechanisms within and across institutions. Sustainability also entails ongoing feedback from stakeholders about the partnership's benefits and impact and recognition of partners, both publicly and privately, of their efforts (The Council for Corporate & School Partnerships, n.d.b.).

Marc Baiocco, Superintendent of Elmsford Union Free School District in Elmsford, New York (also presented in chapter 5), figured out a way to sustain a partnership with a local university that began in 2010. When the partnership began, Marc was the new principal of the district's one junior/

senior high school. His then superintendent wanted to form a PDS with Marc's school so that the students could get additional academic support.

She appealed to Marc to join her in this effort, which he gladly did. Since Marc was focused on improving his school's graduation rate at the time, he thought that the extra help from the university could help him attain his goal. He worked closely with the university to hire a PDS liaison who spent two days each week in the school to work with his teachers and students and supervise student teachers. Marc and the PDS liaison established an after-school program to help his eleventh- and twelfth-grade students pass the statewide mathematics exam needed for graduation. Graduate students who were pursuing a master's degree in secondary mathematics education worked three days each week with Marc's students, who did eventually pass the test.

When Marc discovered two years later that this PDS liaison left the university, he was at a crossroads. He could find someone new or dissolve the partnership. He decided to look for someone new because the partnership had become so valuable for his school. The newly hired PDS liaison worked with Marc to co-sponsor a summer school enrichment program for students in need of additional academic support. Graduate education students worked with his junior high school students to develop English/Language Arts skills through the study of history/social studies.

This PDS liaison began to schedule annual visits to the university so that the eleventh graders could learn about the benefits of attending college. This liaison also worked with the junior high school teachers to help them with program development. He made it a point to attend statewide conferences with the teachers to help them gather information about other successful programs.

In 2017, after spending seven years as the principal, Marc was selected to lead the district as its next superintendent. Marc determined that the principal that he was going to hire to replace himself had to be invested in the PDS model because the partnership helped with his own work in the community. As with other districts in his region, he had seen a steady increase of Hispanic students in his schools. He had become an active partner with the university's Hispanic parent outreach initiative to provide guidance to Hispanic parents on ways to engage with the schools. Marc wanted his new principal to do the same.

Marc has worked hard to sustain his partnership with a local university. It is not the only partnership he has developed and sustained. He knows that he and his staff cannot do it alone. He needs others outside his district to bring expertise to his schools so that, together, they can help his students graduate with the skills needed for college and careers.

He works with partners who share his views about teaching and learning and can adapt to shifts in his district as he adapts to shifts in expectations from his state. He makes it a point to listen and learn from his partners and expects his partners to do the same. He believes that it is worth sustaining valuable partnerships when both parties share the same goals for students (Hammerness, MacPherson Macdonald, Roditi, & Curtis-Bey, 2017).

REASONS FOR *NOT* SUSTAINING PARTNERSHIPS

Not all partnerships can and should be sustained. It is all about the relationship with partners, the deliverables in relation to the goals, and the impact on stakeholders.

Relationship with Partners

Relationships with partners are critical for sustainability. When relationships break down or no longer exist, so do the partnerships. Reasons could include changes in partners or disconcerting discoveries about partners. A chronic problem with partnerships is the change in leadership. People leave jobs, get promoted or demoted to different jobs, or change responsibilities.

Whereas the original partners were enthusiastic, the new partners are lukewarm at best. The original partner might not have communicated with the new partner critical information about the value of the partnership, leaving the new partner with incomplete information about reasons for keeping it as a high priority responsibility. Or, the new partner simply is not inclined to continue the partnership because of different areas of interest.

These new partners might give lip service to their investment in the partnership or, worse yet, abandon the partnership entirely. While these new partners do not hide their apathetic views, there could be others in the partnership organization who can resurrect what existed or start anew. If it is not possible to find someone who is committed to the partnership, it most likely cannot be sustained.

The Director of Special Education in a suburban-rural district in the Midwest had partnered with a local manufacturing company of assistive technology. He and the owner had become professional friends after meeting at a statewide special education conference. The owner offered to create a partnership with the director so that students would have access to some of the most current assistive technology devices.

The business owner was glad to do this because, in addition to helping students with special needs, he could see firsthand how the devices were working. He was able to post online videotapes of the students using the devices, which helped with his own sales. As with any successful partnership, it was a win-win. When the owner retired and passed on the business to his son, the director discovered that the son had no interest in continuing with the partnership. The son did not want to spend the additional funds to supply the district with the technology and did not care about using the students' use of the technology as a marketing tool.

The director knew that no matter what he said or tried to do with the son or anyone else in the company, he had to dissolve the partnership. This same set of circumstances happened to a supervisor of the district's physical education program who had a partnership with a local exercise equipment store that donated all types of equipment. The gym teachers were thrilled each year to receive sporting goods and supplies for their programs and students. They posted signs in the schools' gyms about the generous donation of the equipment and used every opportunity to publicly thank this local store.

They were quite upset when they learned that the new store owner refused to continue with the partnership. The owner felt that the partnership was frivolous and unnecessary for business and sent a notice to the director that the partnership had been dissolved.

Evolving incompatibility with existing partners is another reason why partnerships cannot be sustained. Partners might have thought that they had the same goals or thought that they were kindred spirits to discover a year later that neither was true. Small annoyances might lead to repeated frustrations that cannot be overlooked. Partners stop getting along and, rather than address issues, avoid each other. This discordance interferes with the partnership's progress so severely that the partnership cannot be sustained.

Growing incapability happened to a high school principal who had partnered with a local theater company to bring actors to the school to mentor high school students who were seriously interested in going to drama school and becoming actors. These actors met with the students individually and in small-group settings to help them develop a repertoire of skills across a variety of theatrical genres. The students and their parents were thrilled with this opportunity. The high school drama teacher was not.

She found the actors to be presumptuous and interfering. She did not think that the actors were helping the students, but rather teaching them bad habits. When the principal shared with the theater company director, quite apologetically, the teacher's thoughts, the director agreed to speak with his actors. The director then learned from the actors that they thought that the drama teacher lacked talent and skill. And so began a downward spiral where the principal was defending his teacher and the director was defending his actors. Within six months, the partnership dissolved.

The partners' leaders serve as brokers or boundary spanners who share information with each other and their stakeholders and facilitate the accomplishment of the partnership's goals, even in the face of shifting demands (Yendol-Hoppey et al., 2011). If they cannot get their stakeholders to go along with the partnership's conditions, the partnership cannot survive.

Deliverables in Relation to Goals

If either partner cannot deliver what it is supposed to deliver, the partnership should not exist. Deliverables can be funds, goods, and services. Expected deliverables are written in Memoranda of Understanding (MOU). After a year passes, and there is little or no evidence of either partner upholding its agreement for the partnership, one or both partners should dissolve the agreement.

Examples of the lack of deliverables include companies or community organizations that are not providing promised funds, equipment, materials, or people; or universities that are not sending faculty or students that they pledged to send. Similarly, if schools or districts do not deliver what they agreed to do (e.g., classrooms with willing teachers and students to participate in projects), these are grounds for businesses, community organizations, and universities to sever ties.

A principal who formed a partnership with a local university to provide paid assistantships for graduate students in the elementary education program could not deliver teachers who were willing to mentor the students because his teachers did not want to take time away from their own teaching. He had to sever the agreement, which meant that he had to return to paying more money for teaching assistants who were not as qualified as the graduate students.

Deliverables, whether fiscal or human, determine the success of a partnership. It is the sharing of resources between organizations that enables each to work smarter because opportunities and programs can be expanded (Yendol-Hoppey et al., 2011).

Impact on Stakeholders

Even if partners are compatible and deliverables are in place, partnerships should not continue if there is minimal or no indication of some type of positive impact on stakeholders. Examples for schools can include professional development for teachers, improved standardized test scores for students, safe places for students' for after-school activities, additional mentors for students, coaching for administrators on fiscal management, a development of a technology infrastructure, or increased parent engagement in school activities.

Examples for partners can include the reduction of employee absenteeism, increased service activities, improved morale, improved marketing platforms, or improved literacy skills for employees (The Council for Corporate & School Partnerships, n.d.b.). If both partners find that the goals, as set forth in the MOU, are not being met, even incrementally for the stakeholders, it might not be worthwhile to continue with the partnership.

An elementary school principal, initially quite excited about a partnership with a start-up technology company, had to admit to herself that she needed to end the relationship. The technology company had given her electronic pens for her fifth-grade students to use to help with their spelling. She thought that they were as innovative and useful as advertised. However, after six months, her teachers stopped using them with their students because they were interfering with their spelling development.

While her partners were willing to help in any way and were constantly offering to assist in the classroom, her teachers were consistently reluctant to take advantage of this new technology. At the end of the year, the principal returned the pens to the technology company. Table 7.1 offers questions to ask yourself about your own partnerships to see whether they are worthwhile to continue. If you have answered "no" to more than half of the questions, chances are that the partnership is not worth sustaining.

Table 7.1 Self-Reflective Survey for Sustaining a Partnership

1.	Do I think that the partnership is worthwhile?	Yes	No	Uncertain
2.	Do I enjoy working with my partner?	Yes	No	Uncertain
3.	Do my partner and I have similar goals for the students?	Yes	No	Uncertain
4.	Do my partners' interests continue to be noble?	Yes	No	Uncertain
5.	Are my teachers responding well to the partnership?	Yes	No	Uncertain
6.	Are my parents and the community supportive of the partnership?	Yes	No	Uncertain
7.	Are we accomplishing the goals we set out to accomplish?	Yes	No	Uncertain
8.	Am I able to manage my responsibilities for the partnership?	Yes	No	Uncertain
9.	Is my partner fulfilling his/her responsibilities for the partnership?	Yes	No	Uncertain
10.	Is the partnership having a positive impact on students?	Yes	No	Uncertain

GUIDELINES FOR SUSTAINING PARTNERSHIPS

Partnerships should be sustainable from the start. Strong collaborations require a great deal of effort to start and even more effort to sustain. Organizations must possess the skill and will to develop relationships among various stakeholders (Gooden, Bell, Gonzales, & Lippa, 2011).

Partners who form relationships that sustain themselves understand that they need to take the time to understand each other, reach common goals, identify possible projects, remove potential roadblocks, and put into place workable organizational structures. Partners understand that they cannot rush into signing a MOU without specifying ways in which each will collaborate.

Partners understand that their relationships are works in progress and that they must work through difficulties as they arise. Partners devote time, energy, and resources to each other. They communicate frequently and enthusiastically to each other and have mutual respect for what the other brings to the relationship (Sutton, 2014). They know that they must implement a system for monitoring and assessing progress (Gooden et al., 2011).

Partnerships are instigated because of a need. An example of a partnership that sustained itself for more than a decade was instigated by a large independent, predominantly single sex K-12 boarding and day school with a rural university when the physical education teachers realized that they needed help in addressing their students' motor development.

The school's headmaster reached out to the senior member of the university's physical education department to develop a plan to help assess their students' motor development and figure out ways to help them improve. In addition, the teachers sought to upgrade their own knowledge and skills so that they could provide the type of instruction that would help their students succeed with a movement intervention program.

This partnership helped the students to improve their motor development, the teachers to improve their skills, the university's teacher candidates to learn how to teach, and the university faculty to improve their curriculum in light of what they discovered about teaching in the school. A similarly successful project was undertaken for health education, focused specifically on nutrition. The mutual benefits for all stakeholders have enabled such a program to continue (Miller, Haynes, & Pennington, 2015).

Entrepreneurial Leadership Orientation

Go slow. Spend time dating. Follow your own advice (Kisch, 2014). At the same time do not be browbeat into letting it go. *Rosa Taylor, principal of Park Avenue School in Port Chester, New York, illustrates an entrepreneurial leadership orientation in developing and sustaining partnerships that she has created for her school. She currently has three partnerships, one with Family Services of Westchester, one with Open Door Family Medical Centers, and one with a local university.*

The partnership with Family Services of Westchester augments the work of her school psychologist to provide programs and counseling where needed. The partnership with Open Door Family Medical Centers provides a school-based health center that provides medical care and dental services to the students. Her partnership with the university is in the form of a PDS to help with her teachers' professional development and student learning. She proudly identifies these partnerships on her school's website.

Twice, since she formed a partnership with the university, there was a threat to stop the partnership because she did not have a PDS liaison in place and she did not have the budgetary funds to support her school's partnership in the local PDS network. She did not want to hear it. She wanted her teachers and students to benefit from the learning opportunities that PDS work provided (e.g., student visitations to the college and Lunch 'n Learns for teachers).

Rosa had face-to-face meetings with her assistant superintendent and the university's coordinator, worked collaboratively with another principal in the district to find funds to support PDS work, and sent emails to the university coordinator to find a pathway for the PDS to continue. She would not give up, no matter what others said, because she knew that the PDS was good for her school.

Mutual Understanding and Expectations

You need to want to accomplish similar goals from the partnership. You cannot rush into a partnership without knowing who is in charge and who controls the decisions about the partnership related to programs, personnel, and resources. MOUs are critical for providing explicit statements about roles and responsibilities. DiMartino and Thompson (2016) describe a failed partnership in New York City because stakeholders did not take the time to make the appropriate arrangements.

Being explicit about a partnership's expectations is so critical. When a primary school engaged a professional writer to work with children on an arts project, the teachers and the writer thought that the result would be a lively, publishable product. When the writer worked with the children, he thought that he should use the children's experiences and ideas as a basis for meaningful and engaged composition about hypothetical families that could be published. The result was a text that the head teacher and her staff felt was inappropriate.

The writer and the school had different understandings about "appropriate" projects and "meaningful" projects. Had the school and writer worked this out ahead of time, they could have avoided major conflict. Instead, a purportedly positive experience for the children, teachers, and school turned into a failed project for all involved that could not be sustained (Thomson, Hall, & Russell, 2006).

You need to want the partnership to keep going because you believe that whatever the partnership is providing is helping your students, teachers, and community. You are the critical factor for establishing the feeling with your own constituency and your partner's constituency that there is a mutual benefit or "win-win" situation for both parties to keep the relationship alive. The reciprocal nature of the partnership with a business, a community, or a college/university partner is the standout feature for its potential longevity.

A study of forty different types of community partners at five different types of schools found that the principal's leadership is critical for partners' beliefs in the value of the partnership (Gross et al., 2015).

Multiple types of school–community partners were represented. Partners know when principals have a clear vision and genuine desire to build and sustain a collaborative relationship. Partners also recognize that principals are the ones to create an inviting school culture that has teachers committed to working with partners so that partners feel welcome in the schools.

Constant Communication

As shared in chapters 4 and 6, a key factor for a partnership's success is communication. To sustain a partnership, it is important to communicate and/or meet regularly with your partners to determine how the partnership is going. Meetings can occur in person, by telephone, or through email, text, Skype, or any shared form of social media. Meetings can provide an update of what is working and what still needs improvement, based on evaluation criteria that you and your partner have established. Meetings also can address a specific problem that has arisen.

A middle school principal shared that he had a partnership with a local corporation that offered to provide four employee volunteers to teach after-school computer science classes for his seventh- and eighth-grade students in the school's two computer labs. Forty students could sign up for the 10-week course that would position them to receive a certificate of achievement if they passed the assessment that the corporate employees and teachers had created. The employees were scheduled to team teach the course.

After two weeks, it became obvious that one of the teams was dysfunctional. One team member showed up late and left early while the other team member was apathetic about the entire project. The students soon realized the problem and reported to the after-school staff supervisor what was happening. The principal, who had had previous success with this partner, reached out to his contact through email to explain the situation and schedule a telephone call for the next day to request new employee volunteers. The partner apologized and quickly found two new employees who were enthusiastic about team teaching the course.

This principal knew that the partner would want to help because of the local corporation's public commitment to student success. The principal also knew that it was his responsibility to communicate this snafu so that it could be rectified before it was too late. Both the principal and partner already were planning the end-of-course ceremony for students that involved the local media. Neither wanted questions asked about the uneven success of the two classes.

Communication does not necessarily have to be about the partnership per se, but rather can occur because of the partner's presence in your school. You might want to invite partners to serve on committees and leadership teams to contribute to your school or district's governance decisions. Or, you might want to involve your partners in school tours, projects, field trips, classroom visitations, and school-wide or districtwide events (Gross et al., 2015), based on your partner's availability and interests.

Even when communication fails, start the conversation again. Resume communication and do not blame your partner. If you cannot get an answer from an email, try a telephone call. Be persistent. If you have been inconsistent in responding to your partner, apologize and start again. Do not assume that they are no longer interested.

As Myende (2013) discovered, principals should be the ones who ensure that there is effective communication between their schools and their partners. It does not mean that they have to hold all the power or responsibility. Partnership sustainability is all about the leadership and ways in which the leadership fosters all facets of the collaboration with critical stakeholders.

Continuous Monitoring of Conflicting Expectations

Leaders who monitor their partnerships understand that they need to create an environment that allows for problems to be posed as well as conflict and differences to be discussed, negotiated, and resolved. They understand how to create environments where there is enough trust to have real conversations (Yendol-Hoppey et al., 2011).

Avoid partnership strains because of differences in cultures when it comes to the pace of work, professional focus, career reward structure, or hierarchical differences (see chapter 6). Do what you can to mentor your teachers so that they embrace collaboration and sidestep turf battles. Help teachers to avoid focusing on any negative past experiences with partnerships, get past personality conflicts, and overcome any fears of risk (Gooden et al., 2011).

Facilitation of Two-Way Flow of Activities

Acknowledge that you, as the building or district leader, play a critical role in establishing the vision and expectations for any partnership that you establish with an external organization. Your actions, or inactions, mold the extent to which your school or district is open to partners, the type of partners that you welcome into your building(s), and the expectations for collaboration among partners (Abt Associates, 2016).

Your openness to having partners work with you and your staff from the beginning about developing goals in relation to needs and aligning resources and activities to goals sets the stage for partnership sustainability. Two-way goal setting and planning sessions contribute to establishing a process for the flow of activities from both partners. If three or more partners are involved, it becomes even more critical to establish goals, priorities, and expectations prior to the onset of partnership activities.

A study of a partnership that was formed between five elementary schools in one urban district and seven nonprofit community partners to provide literacy interventions for kindergarten through third grade found that certain elements need to be in place for such partnerships to be sustained. Partners need to have a common agenda, agree on how progress will be measured, shared responsibility for mutually reinforcing activities, efficient and effective communication, and continuous advocacy for the partnership by the district leader (Smith, Ralston, Naegele, & Waggoner, 2019).

As a leader, your authentic buy-in needs to be continuous if the partnership is going to sustain itself. Your constant communication with your stakeholders about the status and benefits of a partnership allows for a smooth flow of activities. If teachers know to expect that their children will participate twice a week with an artist-in-residence, funded by a community partner, teachers can plan for this change in schedule. They can work with the artist-in-residence to identify ways to integrate students' experiences with the artist into the curriculum. Teachers need to know how partners are participating in the schools so that they are prepared for instructional and scheduling shifts.

One way to ensure reciprocity in a partnership is to identify ways that the school can give back to the community (e.g., open building use, participation in service learning projects). At the same time, identify ways to harness community resources and services to support families and children in the school setting (Gross et al., 2015). It is about considering the WIIFMs (What's In It For Me?) and the WIIFTs (What's In It For Them?).

Measures of Success

Assessment is critical for knowing whether the partnership can be sustained. A partnership's ability to be sustained requires constant monitoring and evaluation to know whether partners are collaborating effectively, stakeholders are appropriately involved and satisfied, and students are benefitting as envisioned. The ability to provide some type of empirical data that demonstrates improved outcomes is central to partnership sustainability, especially in the current accountability context of schools (Yendol-Hoppey et al., 2011).

Chapter 3 described the types of assessments that can help to monitor and evaluate a partnership. Chapters 4, 5, and 6 offered examples for assessing the value of specific types of partnerships. Any assessment measure, whether qualitative, quantitative, or a mixed method, should offer partners the opportunity to reflect on the partnership's value and ways that it can be improved if it is worth keeping. For small-scale partnerships, a phone conversation or email exchange between partners might be enough to solidify continuation. For large-scale partnerships, meetings, focus groups, case studies, and surveys are probably needed to delineate measures of success.

Meetings can include pairs of individuals, small groups, or large groups, with a mix of individuals from each partner organization. Case studies can include interviews with key people in the partnership to acquire information about their history with the partnership, involvement with activities, roles and responsibilities, ways in which they have been held accountable, and perceptions of challenges, available resources, achievements, and future possibilities (The Council for Corporate & School Partnerships, n.d.b).

Universities, with their emphasis on scholarship and publication, have access to faculty and administrative staff who are expert in conducting research about partnerships' achievements and sustainability potential. Two studies about school-university partnerships with Australian schools were able to use interviews and surveys to determine the value of these partnerships for teaching of science in the schools, especially with the current focus on STEM (Science Technology Engineering Mathematics) (Jones et al, 2016; Tytler et al., 2015).

Universities also have access to sponsoring agencies that will help to conduct research about partnerships. A large-scale study on the value of more than 250 school-community partnerships to promote arts in education had the funds to use meetings with stakeholders to identify ways to sustain such partnerships. A three-step model emerged: Get Ready, Get Set, Act. During the Get Ready stage, partners got acquainted and built trust by identifying a shared problem or opportunity. During the Get Set stage, partners planned by identifying leadership, developing shared goals, and establishing structures. During the Act stage, partners implemented programs, monitored, and evaluated to help sustain their relationships (Dreeszen, 1992).

All partnerships—whether with universities, communities, or businesses—should be evaluated for their impact; otherwise, why bother? Chances are that your partners will work with you to develop protocols for the partnership when it is large-scale. Your role is to ensure that your stakeholders provide the necessary feedback so that you and your partner have a clear understanding of the partnership's viability.

Your own conversations with stakeholders, coupled with their completion of surveys, participation in focus groups and other evaluation protocols, will contribute to a complete profile of the partnership's value. Any evaluation depends on the scale of the partnership so that you and your partners have the necessary information.

Surveys and questionnaires can be as simple as a few key questions or very comprehensive with hundreds of items related to every partnership component; for example, meetings, roles and responsibilities, operational understandings, rules and procedures, communication mechanisms, sense of ownership, leadership skills, staff expertise, benefits, costs, budget monitoring, decision-making opportunities, activities, outcomes, and barriers (El Ansari, 1999).

Table 7.2 provides sample questions from the survey that a college uses to determine the degree to which the teachers from each of the professional development schools are aware of, involved with, and satisfied with the collaborative work of the partnership. They reveal valuable information from the teachers' perspective. This helps to determine how far reaching the partnership goes, blatant issues with each partnership, and work that still needs to be done to improve the value of the partnership.

CONSIDERATIONS FOR REVISITING AND RENEWING PARTNERSHIPS

Use Outcomes to Determine Short- and Long-Term Opportunities

Outcomes from the assessment will help to determine the type of short-term and long-term opportunities that might be available with the partnership. Many options are available, ranging from leaving it as is to disbanding it entirely. Along this continuum are options such as:

- changing the focus ever so slightly
- redefining roles and responsibilities
- engaging a large number of people from the partner organizations in new ways
- rewriting the partnership agreement or MOU to reflect new goals and new activities
- expanding the partnership with new partners
- developing a termination strategy.

Termination could mean that the purpose of the partnership has been accomplished. It does not necessarily mean that the partnership has failed (The Council for Corporate & School Partnerships, n.d.b).

Table 7.2 Sample Questions from Professional Development School (PDS) Partnership Survey

1. If you have participated in PDS professional development work this past year, please indicate which types:
   - ☐ Lunch and learn
   - ☐ Book club
   - ☐ In-school professional development
   - ☐ In-classroom support
   - ☐ Action research
   - ☐ Local, regional, or statewide professional development conference
   - ☐ National or international professional development conference

2. Please indicate the extent to which you would agree with each of the following statements about the partnership. Circle a number 1–5 for each item, where 1 represents Strongly Disagree (SD), 2 – Disagree (D), 3 – Not Applicable/Not Known (N/A), 4 – Agree (A), 5 – Strongly Agree (SA).

		SD	D	N/A	A	SA
a.	Our partnership includes all members of the school community	1	2	3	4	5
b.	The partnership is mutually beneficial	1	2	3	4	5
c.	Trust exists between the university and our school that enables us to collaborate	1	2	3	4	5
d.	Open communication exists between the university and our school	1	2	3	4	5
e.	Our voices and perspectives are heard	1	2	3	4	5
f.	We celebrate our joint work and accomplishments	1	2	3	4	5
g.	There are sufficient resources to support our work	1	2	3	4	5
h.	We share the same vision with the university for our partnership	1	2	3	4	5

Any of the options mentioned above, other than leaving as is or terminating the agreement, means that you are shifting priorities or repackaging the partnership. Repackaging means that you put the partnership's positive aspects into a more attractive form to generate a new commitment and additional resources (Yendol-Hoppey et al., 2011). For example, you might have discovered that your school's partnership with a children's publishing company to bring authors to your elementary school is not working. The authors are conducting assemblies with too wide an age range of students.

The teachers would prefer an entirely different format, a different set of authors who understand children's differing needs, and new goals for the publishing company's presence in the school. The teachers charge you with repackaging the partnership agreement to shift its purpose. By repackaging the partnership, you help to sustain its usefulness and overall worth.

Co-Construct Next Steps with Partners

Any repackaging effort must be co-constructed with your partner. To facilitate a positive outcome, reach out to your partners as soon as possible so that they do not hear the news from someone else. Be straightforward, honest, and upfront with important information, and explain how any changes to the partnership will improve practices to accommodate changing contexts and changing roles (Yendol-Hoppey et al., 2011).

Work together to identify ways that any repackaging is mutually beneficial. With the example above, and after explaining the teachers' wishes, host a series of meetings that involve the publisher's key persons and your lead teachers. Prepare ahead of time with your teachers a proposal with a suggested plan for changes with the format, authors, and goals. It could be two separate sessions, K-1, 2-3 and 4-5, with authors of books for these grade levels with specific grade-appropriate activities for each set of sessions.

Students as Beneficiaries

Students need to be the beneficiaries, whether directly or indirectly, of every partnership formed. When partnerships are sustainable, it means that they are having some type of positive impact on students. A study of a school-university partnership intended to increase fourth-grade students' awareness of college opportunities and increase university student-athletes' understanding of the needs in the local community has shown great promise for continuation. Student athletes, as part of a service opportunity, went to a local elementary school in a high-needs district to mentor fourth-grade students on a weekly basis about the benefits of going to college.

Each week, student athletes first spent time discussing their college academic and athletic experiences and answering questions from students about the college experience. They then participated with the children in a classroom activity that included reading, math games, or science projects designed by the classroom teacher. The fourth-grade teachers involved with the study reported that their students' participation in the program increased the students' motivation and decreased behavioral issues in the classroom.

The fourth-grade students reported an increased understanding of the college experience through working with the student-athletes. The student athletes saw themselves as leaders and role models. Although there were issues with the reliability of the student-athletes because of games, and mentoring protocols could have been stronger, the overall project was deemed successful enough for all to be continued. The willingness of all parties to communicate about ways to improve the benefits for both parties contributed to its ability to be sustained (Rahill, Norman, & Tomaschek, 2017).

A technical school in Mesa, Arizona, the East Valley Institute for Technology, has formed partnerships with different industries to help their high school and adult students get workforce-ready experiences in one of the thirty-five occupations offered at the school. Partnerships involve advisory committees between the school and the specific industry to help place students for job shadowing and internship opportunities. For their automotive technologies program, they send students to local dealerships to learn the trade.

For their culinary arts program, they have chefs come to the school to prepare a three-course meal to get students started in understanding the restaurant business. They even set aside a parcel of land to have a local healthcare facility lease land to offer medical services and programs for patients. The school's health and nursing students now can have clinical rotations at this on-campus site that they hope can transition to part-time and full-time positions. This school's leadership understands the need to have these partnerships "to help students turn their passion into a paycheck" (Nichols, 2012, p. 39). Textbox 7.1 offers a summary of ideas for sustaining partnerships.

TEXTBOX 7.1 IDEAS FOR SUSTAINING PARTNERSHIPS

1. Value your partner organization, your partner's leader(s), and individuals within the partner organization
2. Appreciate the resources, both human and fiscal, that your partner can offer
3. Communicate and collaborate with your partner frequently and collegially
4. Monitor the progress of your partnership regularly, objectively, and strategically
5. Ensure that the MOU is current and accurate in its description of purpose, roles and responsibilities, policies, procedures, dates of operation, and fiscal obligations
6. Take an active role in making changes to the partnership, based on empirical data.

THE IMPORTANCE OF ENTREPRENEURIAL
LEADERSHIP FOR SUCCESSFUL PARTNERSHIPS

Partnerships are only valuable if they have impact (Jones et al., 2016). Some type of system needs to be put into place to ensure that there is evidence of positive and sustainable impact.

Even though principals and superintendents must adhere to regulations (demands for accountability) and comply with institutional pressures (improve academic achievement), they also have the ability to serve as entrepreneurs who take a proactive role to advance initiatives that help with the needs of their schools. As stated in the previous chapters, entrepreneurs are risk takers, high achievers, and creative problem solvers with their approaches in solving problems and in producing benefits (Fernald, Solomon, & Tarabishy, 2005; Yemini, Addi-Raccah, & Katarivas, 2015).

They have the ability to influence and motivate others, set direction, handle resources strategically, and encourage others to seek opportunities. These leaders are able to bring about change in challenging situations by responding in timely and innovative ways. They have a mindset for seizing opportunities and an energetic spirit for working with others to bring about solutions to problems (Woods, 2013).

Entrepreneurial leaders in schools are motivated by their values and pursue initiatives that have both short-term and long-term worth; in other words, projects that are sustainable. They work with their dedicated team of teachers and administrators and are able to motivate and convince them to pursue entrepreneurial ventures. Because schools are inherently resource poor, they understand that they need partners to provide them with access to funding and resources. They can engage in an ongoing process of responding to opportunities because they have support from their stakeholders (Yemini et al., 2015).

Educational leaders are being pressed to become more entrepreneurial to promote new ideas and new practices and take advantage of opportunities that will help to improve performance in schools. Partnerships with other individuals and institutions help leaders to branch out into new arenas. Although there are claims that educational leaders are not predisposed to this orientation, there are many skills that can and should be developed to help practicing and prospective leaders think, act, and be entrepreneurial.

By assessing your own capacity for assuming roles and skills in establishing and sustaining partnerships, you can develop strategies for improvement so that you can become increasingly more confident with your abilities to be a good partner. You need to see yourself as a champion of partnerships, manager of relationships, mobilizer of resources, planner of programs and projects, communicator, negotiator, mediator, facilitator, and coach. As with any other skill development, your capacity for honestly assessing yourself and your growth will contribute significantly toward your success with partnerships. Undoubtedly, your reward will be unanticipated and unimaginable growth and development with your students and teachers. Better yet, your own level of self-satisfaction for challenging yourself to exceed your own standards for professional performance will amaze you!

References

100 years of community school history. (n.d.). Retrieved from web.utk.edu/~fss/minutes/history.doc.

Abt Associates. (2016, October). *Successful school-based partnerships: What does it take?* Bethesda, MD: Author.

Adams, C. J. (2013, December 3). Cambridge academic program makes inroads in U.S. *Education Week.* Retrieved from https://www.edweek.org/ew/articles/2013/12/04/13cambridge.h33.html.

Alliance for Excellent Education. (2013, January 13). *College and career readiness for all youth: The role of businesses.* Retrieved from https://all4ed.org/webinar-event/college-and-career-readiness-for-all-youth-the-role-of-businesses/.

American Association of Colleges for Teacher Education. (2018). *Even well-established partnerships face challenges.* Retrieved from https://videos.aacte.org/even-well-established-partnerships-face-challenges.

American Association of State Colleges and Universities. (n.d.). *Making partnerships work: Principles, guidelines and advice for public university leaders.* Washington, DC: Author.

American Transmission Company. (2018, August 29). *Cristo Rey students join ATC.* Retrieved from https://www.atcllc.com/whats-current/cristo-rey-students-join-atc/.

Anderson-Butcher, D., Stetler, E. G., & Midle, T. (2006). A case for expanded school-community partnerships in support of positive youth development. *Children & Schools, 28*(3), 155–163.

Araujo, K. (2018, August 20). *New Jersey principal's purchase of washers and dryers for his bullied student is an act of love.* Retrieved from https://www.diversityinc.com/principal-helps-bulliedstudents/?utm_source=WhatCounts&utm_medium=Email&utm_campaign=DI%20Newsletter%201%200820.

Badgett, K. (2016). School-business partnerships: Understanding business perspectives. *School Community Journal, 26*(2), 83–105. Retrieved from https://files.eric.ed.gov/fulltext/EJ1123994.pdf.

Balakrishnan, M. S. (2015, June 15). *Five leadership characteristics that entrepreneurs need.* Retrieved from https://www.entrepreneur.com/article/247062.

Beckman High School. (n.d.) *Perfect attendance programs.* Retrieved from https://www.tustin.k12.ca.us/beckman/resources/perfect-attendance-programs.

Better Beginnings. (2016). *Promoting lifelong health starts at home.* Retrieved from https://www.beginbetter.org/.

Bowen, D. H., & Kisida, B. (2017, March). The art of partnerships: Community resources for arts education. *Phi Delta Kappan, 98*(7), 8–14. Retrieved from https://www.kappanonline.org/art-partnerships-community-resources-arts-education/.

Boys and Girls Clubs of America. (n.d.a). *About us.* Retrieved from https://www.bgca.org.

Boys and Girls Clubs of America. (n.d.b). *Education.* Retrieved from https://www.bgca.org/programs/education.

Boys and Girls Clubs of America. (n.d.c). *Programs.* Retrieved from https://www.bgca.org/programs.

Boy Scouts of America. (2019a). *What is boy scouts BSA?* Retrieved from https://www.scouting.org/scoutsbsa/.

Boy Scouts of America. (2019b). *Programs.* Retrieved from https://www.scouting.org/programs/sea-scouts/.

Breault, R. (2014). Power and perspective: The discourse of professional development school literature. *Asia-Pacific Journal of Teacher Education, 42*(1), 22–35.

Brent, B. O., & Lunden, S. (2009). Much ado about very little: The benefits and costs of school-based commercial activities. *Leadership & Policy in Schools, 8*(3), 307–336. Retrieved from https://doi.org/10.1080/15700760802488619.

Brighouse, H. (2005). Channel one, the anti-commercial principle, and the discontinuous ethos. *Educational Policy, 19*(3), 528–549. Retrieved from https://doi.org/10.1177/0895904805276145.

Brockhaus, R., & Horwitz, P. (1986). The psychology of the entrepreneur. In D. Sexton & R. Smilor (Eds.), *The art and science of entrepreneurship* (pp. 25–48). Cambridge, MA: Ballinger.

Carr, N. (2010). What are you selling? *American School Board Journal, 197*(2), 38–39. Retrieved from https://www.nsba.org/newsroom/american-school-board-journal.

Castle, S., Arenda, R. I., & Rockwood, K. D. (2008). Student learning in a professional development school and a control school. *The Professional Educator, 32*(1), 20–34.

Center for Global Education. (2018). *How schools can successfully partner with local businesses.* Retrieved from https://asiasociety.org/education/how-schools-can-successfully-partner-local-businesses.

Children's Aid. (2019). *History of innovation.* Retrieved from https://www.childrensaidnyc.org/about/history-innovation.

Cline, S. (2018, June 7). *Is summer breaking America's school? How the prolonged summer break is dividing students and costing educators.* Retrieved from https://www.usnews.com/news/education-news/articles/2018-06-07/summer-exacerbates-the-divide-between-rich-and-poor-students.

Coalition of Community Schools. (2016). *What is a community school?* Retrieved from http://www.communityschools.org/aboutschools/what_is_a_community_school.aspx.
Coalition for Community Schools at the Institute for Educational Leadership. (2019a). *Developing a vision and strategic plan*. Retrieved from http://www.communityschools.org/resources/buidling_a_vision_and_strategic_plan.aspx.
Coalition for Community Schools at the Institute for Educational Leadership. (2019b). *What is a community school?* Retrieved from http://www.communityschools.org/aboutschools/faqs.aspx.
Coburn, A., & McCafferty, P. (2016). The real Olympic games. *Taboo: The Journal of Culture & Education, 15*(1), 23–40. Retrieved from https://doi.org/10.31390/taboo.15.1.05.
Collaborative Center for Health Equity. (n.d.) *Memorandum of understanding*. Retrieved from https://cche.wisc.edu/research-technical-assistance/resources/.
Cristo Rey Jesuit. (2016). *Meet our local partners*. Retrieved from http://www.cristoreymilwaukee.org/work-study-partners/our-partners/.
Daily, N. L., Swain, L. P., Huysman, M., & Tarrant, C. (2010). America's consumerocracy: No safe haven. *English Journal, 99*(3), 37–41. Retrieved from http://www.ncte.org/journals/ej/issues/v99-3.
D'Ambrosio, L. (2018, March/April). Pastors and principals? You bet!: How hosting a pastors' breakfast can build community connections. *Principals*, 52–53.
Davis, M. R., & Molnar, M. (2014, July 31). Principals test entrepreneurial ideas in K-12. *Education Week*. Retrieved from https://www.edweek.org/ew/aricles/2014/07/37/37principals.h33.html.
DiMartino, C., & Thompson, E. (2016). Partners or managers? A case study of public–private partnerships in New York City. *Journal of Cases in Educational Leadership, 19*(4), 16–31. Retrieved from https://doi.org/10.1177/1555458916672706.
Dreeszen, C. (1992). *Intersections: Community arts and education collaborations* (Report No. ISBN-0945-464096). Washington, DC: John F. Kennedy Center for the Performing Arts, National Assembly of Local Arts, National Endowment for the Arts. (ERIC Document Reproduction Service No. ED 368 606).
Dryfoos, J., & Maguire, S. (2002). *Inside full-service community schools*. Thousand Oaks, CA: Corwin Press.
Duckworth, A. (2016). *Grit: The power of passion and perseverance*. New York: Scribner.
Duncan, R. (1976). The ambidextrous organization: Designing dual structures for innovation. In R. H. Killman, L. R. Rondy, D. Sleven (Eds.), *The management of organization* (pp. 167–188). New York: North Holland.
Eargle, J. C. (2013). "I'm not a bystander": Developing teacher leadership in a rural school-university collaboration. *The Rural Educator, 35*(1), 23–33.
Education World. (1996–2019). *School-business partnerships that work: Success stories form schools of all sizes*. Retrieved from https://www.educationworld.com/a_admin/admin/admin323.shtml.
Edwards, P. A., Domke, L., & White, K. (2017). Closing the parent gap in changing school districts. In S. B. Wepner & D. W. Gómez (Eds.), *Challenges facing*

suburban schools: Promising responses to changing student populations (pp. 109–121). Lanham, MD: Rowman & Littlefield.

El Ansari, W. (1999). *A study of the characteristics, participant perceptions and predictors of effectiveness in community partnerships in health personnel education: The case of South Africa* (Doctoral dissertation). University of Wales College, Newport, United Kingdom.

Engeln, J. T. (2003, March). Guiding school/business partnerships. *Education Digest, 68*(7), 36–40.

Epstein, J. L. (1995). School/family/community partnerships. *Phi Delta Kappan, 76*(9), 701–713.

Epstein, J. L. (2010, November). School/family/community partnerships. *Kappan Classic, 92*(3), 81–96. Retrieved from https://doi.org/10.1177/003172171009200326.

EY. (n.d.). *College MAP.* Retrieved from https://eycollegemap.chronus.com/p/p29/pages/programs.

Farber, S. (2009). *Greater than yourself: The ultimate lesson of true leadership.* New York: Doubleday.

Fernald, L., Solomon, G. T., & Tarabishy, A. (2005). A new paradigm: Entrepreneurial leadership. *Southern Business Review, 30*(2), 1–10.

Ferrara, J., & Gómez, D. W. (2014). Broadening the scope of PDS liaisons' roles in community schools. *School-University Partnerships: The Journal of the National Association for Professional Development Schools, 7*(1), 110–117.

Finkel, E. (2013, October 9). 10 tips for starting your own school-business partnership. *District Administration.* Retrieved from https://www.districtadministration.com/article/10-tips-starting-your-own-school-business-partnership.

Future Teachers of America. (n.d.a). *Home.* Retrieved from http://www.futureteachers.org/index.html.

Future Teachers of America. (n.d.b). *High schools.* Retrieved from http://www.futureteachers.org/Schools.html.

Gilles, C., Wilson, J., & Elias, M. (2009). School-university partnership: Perceptions of the teachers. *School-University Partnerships: The Journal of the National Association for Professional Development Schools, 3*(1), 100–112.

Girl Scouts of the United States of America. (2016–2019a). *Cadettes build sensory tool for children with autism.* Retrieved from https://www.girlscouts.org/en/about-girl-scouts/our-stories/girl-scouts/take-action/cadettes-use-cookie-money-to-build-sensory-tool-for-children-with-autism.html#story$$$/content/gsusa/en/our-stories/girl-scouts.html.

Girl Scouts of the United States of America. (2016–2019b). *Take the lead like a girl scout!* Retrieved from https://www.girlscouts.org/en/about-girl-scouts/like-a-girl-scout.html.

Girl Scouts of the United States of America. (2016–2019c). *The girl scout difference.* Retrieved from https://www.girlscouts.org/en/about-girl-scouts/the-girl-scout-difference.html.

Girl Scouts of the United States of America. (2016–2019d). *Our programs.* Retrieved from https://www.girlscouts.org/en/our-program/our-program.html.

Gómez, D. W., Wepner, S. B, & Quatroche, D. (2017, March). *University leadership in professional development schools.* Paper presented at the meeting of the American Association of Colleges for Teacher Education, Tampa, FL.

Gómez, D. W., Wepner, S. B, & Quatroche, D. (2019, March). *School-based leadership perspectives on university partnerships.* Paper presented at the meeting of the American Association of Colleges for Teacher Education, Baltimore, MD.

Gooden, M. A., Bell, C. M., Gonzales, R. M., & Lippa, A. P. (2011). Planning university-urban district partnerships: Implications for principal preparation programs. *Educational Planning, 20*(2), 1–13. Retrieved from http://librda.mville.edu:2048/login?url=http://search.ebscohost.com/login.aspx?direct=true&db=ehh&AN=77051588&site=ehost-live.

Grand Pré, P. (2017). *Image, sound, and story: 2017 professional development & open house.* Retrieved from https://education.burnsfilmcenter.org/education/blog/image-sound-and-story-summer-professional-development-registration-is-open.

Gray, B. (2004). Strong opposition: Frame-based resistance to collaboration. *Journal of Community and Applied Social Psychology, 14,* 166–176.

Gregory, A. (2018, March 19). Essential tips for writing an effective elevator pitch. *The balance small business.* Retrieved from https://www.thebalancesmb.com/writing-effective-elevator-pitch-2951691.

Gross, J. M. S., Haines, S. J., Hill, C., Francis, G. L., Blue-Banning, M., & Turnbull, A. P. (2015). Strong school-community partnerships in inclusive schools are "part of the fabric of the school....we count on them." *School Community Journal, 25*(2), 9–34. Retrieved from http://librda.mville.edu:2048/login?url=http://search.ebscohost.com/login.aspx?direct=true&db=ehh&AN=112318839&site=ehost-live.

Hamel, F. L., & Ryken, A. E. (2010). Rehearsing professional roles in community: Teacher identity development in a school-university partnership. *Teacher Development, 14*(3), 335–350.

Hammerness, K., MacPherson, A., Macdonald, M., Roditi, H., & Curtis-Bey, L. (2017). What does it take to sustain a productive partnership in education? *Phi Delta Kappan, 99*(1), 15–20.

Hands on the Land Network. (2001–2019). *About hands on the land.* Retrieved from https://www.handsontheland.org/about-us.html.

Hatch, T. (1998, May). How community contributes to achievement. *Educational Leadership, 55*(8), 16–19.

Hatch, T. (2009). The outside-inside connection. *Educational Leadership, 67*(2), 16–21.

Henrico County School District. (2016, August). *Henrico schools partnership agreement form.* Retrieved from http://henricoschools.us/pdf/Community/PartnershipAgreement.pdf.

Hentschke, G. C. (2009). Entrepreneurial leadership. In B. Davies (Ed.), *The essentials of school leadership* (2nd ed., pp. 147–164). Los Angeles, CA: Sage Publications.

Hernandez-Gantes, V. M., Brookins, S. J., & Fletcher, Jr., E. C. (2017). Promoting active and sustained school-business partnerships: An exploratory case study of an IT academy. *Journal of Research in Technical Careers, 1*(2), 26–35. Retrieved from https://digitalscholarship.unlv.edu/cgi/viewcontent.cgi?article=1023&context=jrtc.

Hess, F. M., & McShane, M. (2016, May). Entrepreneurship as empowerment. *U.S. News & World Report*. Retrieved from https://www.usnews.com/opinion/articles/2016-05-17/embracing-entrepreneurship-as-a-crucial-ally-to-k-12-education.

Hirsch, S. E., Ely, E., Lloyd, J. W. & Isley, D. (2018). Targeted professional development: A data-driven approach to identifying educators' need. *School-University Partnerships: The Journal of the National Association for Professional Development Schools, 11*(2), 84–91.

Hogan, A., Enright, E., Stylianou, M., & McCuaig, L. (2018). Nuancing the critique of commercialisation in schools: Recognising teacher agency. *Journal of Education Policy, 33*(5), 617–631. Retrieved from https://doi.org/10.1080/02680939.2017.1394500.

Hopkins, D. (2011). The value of partnerships. In S. B. Wepner & D. Hopkins (Eds.), *Collaborative leadership in action: Partnering for success in schools* (pp. 7–26). New York: Teachers College Press.

Hovda, R. A. (1999). Working on a public school calendar: Personal reflections on the changing role of a university faculty member in a professional development school. *Peabody Journal of Education, 74*(3/4), 85–93.

Institute for Educational Leadership. (2011). *Glencliff high school metro Nashville public schools Nashville, Tennessee*. Retrieved from http://www.communityschools.org/assets/1/AssetManager/Glencliff%20CS%20Awards%20Brief.pdf.

James, J. H., Kobe, J., Shealey, G., Roretich, R., & Sabatini, E. (2015). Authentic collaborative inquiry: Initiating and sustaining partner research in the PDS setting. *School-University Partnerships: The Journal of the National Association for Professional Development Schools, 8*(2), 53–61.

Jones, M., Hobbs, L., Kenny, J., Campbell, C., Chittleborough, G., Gilbert, A., … Redman, C. (2016). Successful university-school partnerships: An interpretive framework to inform partnership practice. *Teaching & Teacher Education, 60*, 108–120. https://doi.org/10.1016/j.tate.2016.08.006.

Kaplan, G. R. (1996). Profits r us. *Phi Delta Kappan, 78*(3), 1–12. Retrieved from https://www.jstor.org/stable/i20405742.

Karikehalli, S. (2019, June 13). *Delhi sixth-graders build structure for playground*. Retrieved from https://www.thedailystar.com/news/local_news/delhi-sixth-graders-build-playground-gator/article_324e653a-1dde-5df3-b6ec-af66244c9f9d.html.

Keenan & Associates. (2019). *Communities*. Retrieved from https://www.keenan.com/About/Community.

Kisch, M. (2014, May/June). Avoiding the pitfalls of partnerships. *International Educator, 66*–69. Retrieved from https://www.nafsa.org/_/File/_/ie_mayjun14_partner.pdf.

Kiwanis International. (2019). *Our mission*. Retrieved from https://www.kiwanis.org/about/missionccc.

Kurshan, B. (2017, February 1). The necessary mindsets of education entrepreneurs. *Forbes*. Retrieved from https://www.forbes.com/sites/barbarakurshan/2017/02/01/the-necessary-mindsets-of-education-entrepreneurs/#2e9134546879.

Ledoux, M. W., & McHenry, N. (2008). Pitfalls of school-university partnerships. *The Clearing House, 81*(4), 155–165.

Little, P. (2013). School community learning partnerships: Essential to expanded learning success. In T. K. Peterson (Ed.), *Expanding minds and opportunities: Leveraging the power of afterschool and summer learning for student success* (n.p.). Washington, DC: Collaborative Communications Group. Retrieved from https://www.expandinglearning.org/sites/default/files/em_articles/6_schoolcommunitylearning.pdf.

Luxottica. (2014, January 20). *"We help students to see a brighter future" –Luxottica student mentoring program wins award in the United States*. Retrieved from http://www.luxottica.com/en/we-help-students-see-brighter-future-luxottica-student-mentoring-program-wins-award-united-states.

Lynch, M. (2016a, August 7). 4 major types of educational leadership. *The Edvocate*. Retrieved from https://www.theedadvocate.org/4-major-types-of-educational-leadership/.

Lynch, M. (2016b, August 17). Parallels between entrepreneurial traits and school leadership. *The Edvocate*. Retrieved from https://www.theedadvocate.org.

Lynch, M. (2018, April 21). Entrepreneurial leadership: What schools can learn from business leaders. *The Edvocate*. Retrieved from http://www.theedadvocate.org/entrepreneurial-leadership-what-schools-can-learn-from-business-leaders/.

MacDonald, M. F., & Dorr, A. (2005). *Inside school-university partnerships: Successful collaborations to improve high school student achievement*. Los Angeles, CA: Building Educational Success Through (BEST) Collaboration in Los Angeles County. Retrieved from http://apep.gseis.ucla.edu/bestla/BEST-InsideSchlUnivPartnerships.pdf.

Masumato, M., & Brown-Welty, S. (2009). Case study of leadership practices and school-community interrelationships in high-performing, high-poverty, rural California high school. *Journal of Research in Rural Education, 24*(1), 1–18.

McCollum, S. (2005). Should schools court corporate sponsors? No, schools should reject corporate sponsorships in order to protect educational integrity. *Literary Cavalcade, 57*(5), 18–19. Retrieved from http://teacher.scholastic.com/writeit/cavalcade/pdf/feb2005/debate_p18_19.pdf.

McCoy, D. P. (2018, October 16). How a new career program has put these Indianapolis students to work as nursing assistants. *Chalkbeat*. Retrieved from https://www.chalkbeat.org/posts/in/2018/10/16/how-a-new-career-program-has-put-these-indianapolis-students-to-work-as-nursing-assistants/.

McFadden, J. (2016, December 28). *7 big companies giving back to schools in big ways*. Retrieved from https://www.weareteachers.com/7-big-companies-giving-back-schools-big-ways/.

McGrath, R. G., & MacMillan, I. C. (2000). *The entrepreneurial mindset: Strategies for continuously creating opportunity in an age of uncertainty*. Boston, MA: Harvard Business School Press.

McTighe, J., & Wiggins, G. (2005). *Understanding by design*. New York: Pearson.

MENTOR: The National Mentoring Partnership. (2019). *Community engagement*. Retrieved from https://www.mentoring.org/get-involved/community-engagement/.

References

Miller, J., Haynes, J., & Pennington, J. (2015). A partnership aimed at improving health and physical education at a rural school: Impacts on pupils, university students, teachers and academics. *Australian & International Journal of Rural Education, 25*(2), 56–72.

Milner IV, H. R. (2015). *Rac(e)ing to class: Confronting poverty and race in schools and classrooms.* Cambridge, MA: Harvard Education Press.

Molnar, A. (2003). School commercialism hurts all children, ethnic minority group children most of all. *Journal of Negro Education, 72*(4), 371–378. Retrieved from https://doi.org/10.2307/3211189.

Moore, A. (2007). A balancing act. *American School Board Journal, 194*(5), 28–30. Retrieved from https://www.nsba.org/newsroom/american-school-board-journal.

Mount, I. (2010, December/January) Nature vs. nurture: Are great entrepreneurs born ... or made? *Fortune Small Business, 10,* 25–26.

Murfreesboro News and Radio. (2017, October 31). *Nearly 300 RCS students tour various industry sites through chamber partnership.* Retrieved from https://www.wgnsradio.com/nearly-300-rcs-students-tour-various-industry-sites-through-chamber-partnership-cms-42277.

Murphy, J., & Shipman, N. (1999). The interstate school leaders' licensure consortium: A standards-based approach to strengthening educational leadership. *International of Personnel Evaluation in Education, 13*(3), 1–19.

Myende, P. E. (2013). Sustaining school-community partnerships through effective communication. *Communitas, 18,* 76–94.

National Alliance for Youth Sports. (2019a). *Frequently asked questions.* Retrieved from https://www.nays.org/about/about-nays/faqs/.

National Alliance for Youth Sports. (2019b). *Hook a kid on golf.* Retrieved from https://nays.org/programs/hook-a-kid-on-golf/.

National Alliance for Youth Sports. (2019c). *Programs.* Retrieved from https://www.nays.org/programs/.

National Alliance for Youth Sports. (2019d). *Ready, set, run*! Retrieved from https://www.nays.org/programs/ready-set-run/overview/.

National Alliance for Youth Sports. (2019e). *Start smart.* Retrieved from https://www.nays.org/programs/start-smart/overview/.

National Association for Professional Development Schools. (2008). *What it means to be a Professional Development School.* Retrieved from https://napds.org/wp-content/uploads/2014/10/Nine-Essentials.pdf.

National Association for Professional Development Schools. (2019). *9 Essentials.* Retrieved from https://napds.org/nine-essentials/.

National Association of Secondary School Principals (2002). *Strategic partnerships.* Retrieved from https://www.nassp.org/partners-advertisers/strategic-partnerships/.

National Council for Accreditation of Teacher Education. (2001a). *Standards for professional development schools.* Washington, DC: Author.

National Council for Accreditation of Teacher Education. (2001b). *Handbook for assessment of professional development schools.* Washington, DC: Author.

National 4-H. (1902–2019a). *Rural youth development.* Retrieved from https://4-h.org/parents/civic-engagement/rural-youth-development/.

National 4-H. (1902–2019b). *What is 4-H?* Retrieved from https://4-h.org/about/what-is-4-h.

Neck, H. M., Greene, P. G., & Brush, C. G. (2014, August 13). *What managers need to know about entrepreneurship history.* Retrieved from http://www.babson.edu/executive-education/thought-leadership/entrepreneurship/Pages/entrepreneurship-history.aspx.

New Brunswick Rotary Club. (2002–2019). *Schools.* Retrieved from https://newbrunswickrotary.org/page/impact-schools.

Nichols, T. (2012). Public-private partnerships: Benefit students and industry. *Techniques: Connecting Education & Careers, 87*(2), 36–39. Retrieved from http://librda.mville.edu:2048/login?url=http://search.ebscohost.com/login.aspx?direct=true&db=ehh&AN=75328136&site=ehost-live.

Northside Independent School District. (2015, January 15). *Capital group recognized for extraordinary commitment to Ross MS students* Retrieved from https://nisd.net/news/articles/54133.

Nvidia. (n.d.). *About us.* Retrieved from https://www.nvidia.com/en-us/foundation/programs/project-inspire/.

Open Door Family Medical Center and Foundation. (n.d.a). *About us.* Retrieved from https://www.opendoormedical.org/about-us/mission-vision-values/.

Open Door Family Medical Center and Foundation. (n.d.b). *Services.* Retrieved from https://www.opendoormedical.org/services/school-based-health-centers/.

O'Sullivan, M. (2001). *Community mapping: Toward cultural awareness.* Unpublished manuscript prepared for the UNITE workgroup on Pre-service Teacher Education Programs for Urban Schools.

Partners for success. (n.d.). *Our partners.* Retrieved from http: //www.partnerforstudentsuccess.org/.

Pennington, B. (2005). The gym is brought to you by…. *New York Times Upfront, 137*(10), 25. Retrieved from http://link.galegroup.com/apps/doc/A128791195/AONE?u=nysl_me_manhaclb&sid=AONE&xid=ffd67d9c.

Phillips, A. M., & Kohli, S. (2016, December 18). One solution to failing K-12 schools? Let universities help. *Los Angeles Times.* Retrieved from http://www.latimes.com/local/education/la-me-edu-university-partnerships-20161202-story.html.

Platt, R., & Brissett-Kruger, M. (2015, February 17). Program spotlight: "Reading friends" initiative pairs retirees with young students. *School Library Journal.* Retrieved from https://www.slj.com/2015/02/programs/program-spotlight-reading-friends-initiative-pairs-retirees-with-young-students/.

Polly, D., Diegmann, D., Kennedy, P., Brigman, D., & Luce, C. (2019). Rethinking the student teaching internship: The Teacher Education Institute (TEI). *PDS Partners: Bridging Research to Practice, 14*(1), 20–22.

Rahill, S. A., Norman, K., & Tomaschek, A. (2017). Mutual benefits of university athletes mentoring elementary students: Evaluating a university-school district partnership. *School Community Journal, 27*(1), 283–305.

Remillard, J. (2001). *Studying neighborhoods in learning to teach.* Unpublished manuscript prepared for the UNITE workgroup on Pre-service Teacher Education Programs for Urban Schools.

Richardson Chamber of Commerce. (2017). *Connection with education*. Retrieved from (https://www.richardsonchamber.com/connect-with-education/.

Roebuck, C. (2011, December 11). *Critical need for entrepreneurial leaders during turbulent times*. Retrieved from http://www.chrisroebuck.co/critical-need-for-entrepreneurial-leaders-during-turbulent-times/.

Royal, M. (2019, April 18). UAB professor brings science and fun to local elementary school students. *People of UAB*. Retrieved from https://www.uab.edu/news/people/item/10384-uab-professor-brings-science-and-fun-to-local-elementary-school-students?tmpl=component&print=1.

Russell, J. F., & Flynn, R. B. (2000). Commonalities across effective collaboration. *Peabody Journal of Education, 75*(3), 196–204.

Rutherford County Chamber of Commerce. (2014). *Building tomorrow's workforce*. Retrieved from https://rutherfordworks.com/building-tomorrow-s-workforce/programs.

Sanderlin, J. L. (2018, August 16). *Why not? How to build innovative community partnerships*. Retrieved from https://www.naesp.org/blog/why-not-how-build-innovative-community-partnerships.

Sanders, M. G. (2001). A study of the role of "community" in comprehensive school, family and community partnership programs. *The Elementary School Journal, 102*(1), 19–34.

Sanders, M. G., & Lewis, K. C. (2005, February/March). Building bridges toward excellence: Community involvement in high school. *High School Journal, 88*(3), 1–9.

Santiago, D., Ferrara, J., & Quinn, J. (2012). *Whole child, whole school: Applying theory to practice in a community school*. Lanham, MD: Rowman & Littlefield.

Sarasvathy, S. (n.d.) *What makes entrepreneurs entrepreneurial?* Retrieved from http://www.effectuation.org/sites/default/files/research_papers/what-makes-entrepreneurs-entrepreneurial-sarasvathy_0.pdf.

Sawchuck, S. (2018, February 21). In age of high tech, old-school Cambridge curriculum makes unlikely gains. *Education Week*. Retrieved from https://www.edweek.org/ew/articles/2018/02/21/in-age-of-high-tech-old-school-cambridge.html.

Schlesinger, L. A., Kiefer, C. F., & Brown, P. B. (2012, March). New project? Don't analyze-act. *Harvard Business Review*. Retrieved from https://hbr.org/2012/03/new-project-dont-analyze-act.

Schwartz, K. (2018, June 5). How passion projects and community partners create relevant learning for teens in school. *Mindshift*, Retrieved from https://www.kqed.org/mindshift/50974/how-passion-projects-and-community-partners-create-relevant-learning-for-teens-in-school.

Shaw, D. (2000). Critics denounce ZapMe! and its constant commercials. *Curriculum Administrator, 36*(4), 15. Retrieved from http://connection.ebscohost.com/c/articles/3012106/critics-denounce-zapme-constant-commercials.

Sheninger, E. (2010, June 10). Tips for establishing meaningful partnerships. *A principal's reflections: Reflections on teaching, learning, and leadership*. Retrieved from https://esheninger.blogspot.com/2010/06/tips-for-establishing-meaningful.html.

Sherman, E. (2017, August 21). 7 essential tips for a good elevator pitch. *Inc.* Retrieved from https://www.inc.com/erik-sherman/7-essential-tips-for-a-good-elevator-pitch.html.

Shive, R. J. (1984, Summer). School and university partnerships: Meeting common needs. *Improving College and University Teaching, 32*(1), 119–122.

Sirotnik, K. A. (1991). *Making school-university partnerships work.* Retrieved from https://journals.iupui.edu/index.php/muj/article/download/19177/19012/0.

Sloan, W. M. (2008). Collaborating over coffee. *Education Update, 50*(5), 1–7. Retrieved from http://librda.mville.edu:2048/login?url=http://search.ebscohost.com/login.aspx?direct=true&db=ehh&AN=34965806&site=ehost-live.

Smith, R. (2010). The importance of allies. *School Administrator, 67*(6), 23.

Smith, R., Ralston, N., Naegele, Z., & Waggoner, J. (2019). Connecting the classroom and the community: Exploring the collective impact of one district-community partnership. *Educational Forum, 83*(1), 44–59. https://doi.org/10.1080/00131725.2018.1505990.

South Washington County School District. (n.d.). *Toolkit for building partnerships between schools and business or organization South Washington County Schools.* Retrieved from https://docplayer.net/5550265-Toolkit-for-building-partnerships-between-schools-and-businesses-or-organizations-across-south-washington-county-schools.html.

Staff Reports. (2018, October). Sorority donates school supplies. *Suffolk News-Herald.* Retrieved from https://www.suffolknewsherald.com/2018/10/12/sorority-donates-school-supplies/.

Strier, R. (2011). The construction of university-community partnerships: Entangled perspectives. *Higher Education, 62,* 81–97.

Strier, R. (2014). Fields of paradox: University-community partnerships. *Higher Education, 68,* 155–165.

Sullivan, T. (2018, February 26). Rating the clip-and-save fundraisers. *PTO Today.* Retrieved from https://www.ptotoday.com/pto-today-articles/article/55-rating-the-clip-and-save-fundraisers.

Sutton, S. B. (2014, May-June). Make partnerships sustainable from the start. *International Educator,* pp. 66. Retrieved from https://www.nafsa.org/_/File/_/ie_mayjun14_partner.pdf.

Tarasawa, B., Ralson, N. C., & Waggoner, J. (2016). Leveraging university-school district research partnerships: Exploring the longitudinal effects of an early kindergarten transition program. *Journal of Applied Research on Children: Informing Policy for Children at Risk, 7*(1), 1–15. Retrieved from https://pilotscholars.up.edu/cgi/viewcontent.cgi?article=1052&context=edu_facpubs.

The Council for Corporate & School Partnerships. (n.d.a) *Guiding principles for business and school partnerships.* Retrieved from https://cdn.ymaws.com/stem.sfaz.org/resource/resmgr/CCSPGuide.pdf.

The Council for Corporate & School Partnerships. (n.d.b) *A how-to guide for school-business partnerships.* Retrieved from http://www.nhscholars.org/School-Business%20How_to_Guide.pdf.

Thomson, P., Hall, C., & Russell, L. (2006). An arts project failed, censored or … ? A critical incident approach to artist–school partnerships. *Changing English: Studies in Culture & Education, 13*(1), 29–44. Retrieved from https://doi.org/10.1080/1 3586840500523471.

Trachtman, R. (2007). Inquiry and accountability in professional development schools. *The Journal of Educational Research, 100*(4), 197–204.

Tytler, R., Symington, D., Williams, G., White, P., Campbell, C., Chittleborough, G.,…Dziadkiewicz, N. (2015). *Building productive partnerships for STEM Education: Evaluating the model & outcomes of the scientists and mathematicians in schools program 2015*. Geelong, Australia: Deakin University.

United Way. (2019a). *The future of philanthropy is here*. Retrieved from https://www.unitedway.org/.

United Way. (2019b). *Our impact*. Retrieved from https://www.unitedway.org/our-impact/.

University of Delaware. (2017, November 17). *Partnership for public education. Mechanical engineering student squad*. Retrieved from https://sites.udel.edu/ppe/2017/11/17/mechanical-engineering/.

USAscholarships.com. (2019). *The NFIB young entrepreneur awards program*. Retrieved from https://usascholarships.com/the-nfib-young-entrepreneur-awards-program/.

Venkataraman, S., Sarasvathy, S. D., Dew, N., & Forster, W. R. (2012). Reflection on the 2010 AMR decade award: Whither the promise? Moving forward with entrepreneurship as a science of the artificial. *Academy of Management Review, 37*(1), 21–33.

Vesper, K. H., & Gartner, W. B. (1997). Measuring progress in entrepreneurship education. *Journal of Business Venturing, 12*(5), 403–421.

Viadero, D. (2009). Commercialism in schools. *Education Week, 29*(7), 4–5. Retrieved from https://www.edweek.org/ew/articles/2009/10/14/07report-2.h29.html.

Walsh, M. E., & Backe, S. (2013). School-university partnerships: Reflections and opportunities. *Peabody Journal of Education, 88*(5), 594–601.

Warby Parker. (n.d.). *Pupils project collection*. Retrieved from https://www.warbyparker.com/pupils-project.

Weisman, J. (1991). PTA principles on corporate support fail to win over other organizations. *Education Week, 10*(40), 10. Retrieved from https://www.edweek.org/ew/articles/1991/07/31/10350063.h10.html.

Weller, C. (2016, August 16). *Whirlpool gave washers and dryers to 17 schools in Illinois and California and attendance rates shot up –here's why*. Retrieved from https://www.businessinsider.com/washing-machines-solve-schools-big-problem-2016-8.

Wepner, S. B. (2014). Developing partnerships through collaboration to promote professional development. In S. Kragler, L. Martin, K. L. Bauserman, & D. Quatroche (Eds.), *The handbook of professional development, PK-12: Successful models and practice* (pp. 339–358). New York: Guilford.

Wepner, S. B., Ferrara, J., Rainville, K. N., Gómez, D. W., Lang, D. E., & Bigaouette, L. (2012). *Changing suburbs, changing students: Helping school leaders face the challenges*. Thousand Oaks, CA: Corwin.

Wepner, S. B., Gómez, D. W., Cunningham, K. E., Rainville, K. N., & Kelly, C. (2016). *Literacy leadership in changing schools: 10 keys to successful professional development.* New York: Teachers College Press.

Wikipedia. (2019a). *List of social fraternities and sororities.* Retrieved from https://en.wikipedia.org/wiki/List_of_social_fraternities_and_sororities.

Wikipedia. (2019b). *Social services.* Retrieved from https://en.wikipedia.org/wiki/Social_services.

Woods, P. A. (2013). Sense of purpose: Reconfiguring entrepreneurialism in public education. In C. L. Slater & S. W. Nelson (Eds.), *Understanding the principalship: An international guide to principal preparation. Advances in educational administration, vol. 19* (pp. 223–241). Bingley, UK: Emerald Group Publishing Limited.

Yemini, M., Addi-Raccah, A., & Katarivas, K. (2015). I have a dream. *Educational Management Administration & Leadership, 43*(4), 526–540. https://doi.org/10.1177/1741143214523018.

Yendol-Hoppey, D., Hoppey, D., & Price, T. (2011). Sustaining partnerships. In S. B. Wepner & D. Hopkins (Eds.), *Collaborative leadership in action: Partnering for success in schools* (pp. 74–96). New York: Teachers College Press.

About the Authors

Shelley B. Wepner is dean and professor of Education in the School of Education of Manhattanville College, Purchase, New York. Shelley was a K-8 teacher and administrator in three school districts in New Jersey before becoming a faculty member and administrator at William Paterson University and then at Widener University. Shelley has been involved in partnership work since the 1980s. She served as a faculty and administrative university liaison to urban and suburban professional development schools at the elementary, middle-school, and high school levels.

Since 2004, when she became dean at Manhattanville College, she has worked with principals and superintendents to form and sustain a network of professional development schools that are part of the School of Education's Changing Suburbs Institute® (CSI). She also has worked with private and public schools, teacher centers, and regional and staff-affiliated organizations to form different types of partnerships.

Shelley has published more than 150 articles, books, book chapters, and award-winning software packages focused on K-12 education and higher education connections and leadership skills in teacher education and literacy development. Her most recent coedited book is *Challenges Facing Suburban Schools: Promising Responses to Changing Student Populations* (Rowman & Littlefield, 2017). She also coedited *The Administration and Supervision of Reading Programs, 5th Edition* (Teachers College Press, 2014) as well as all prior editions.

Shelley and her colleagues were awarded the Jerome L. Neuner Award for Excellence in Professional-Scholarly Publication from the American Association of University Administrators in June 2018 for their publication of "Education Deans' Beliefs about Essential Ways of Thinking, Being, and Acting: A National Survey."

She was awarded the 2019 Educator of the Year Award by the University of Pennsylvania Graduate School of Education Alumni Association, where she received her master's and doctoral degrees.

Diane W. Gómez is associate professor of Second Languages and chairperson for the Department of Educational Foundations and Special Subjects at Manhattanville College, Purchase, New York. Diane is a former high school Spanish teacher, and has taught ESOL and special education. She has served as a Professional Development School (PDS) liaison for two of Manhattanville College School of Education's Changing Suburbs Institute® (CSI) partnership schools, and is a member of Manhattanville's CSI Advisory Board.

Her research interests include multicultural and multilingual education and leadership in field-based settings of full-service community and professional development schools. She has coauthored or coedited three CSI related books, *Challenges Facing Suburban Schools: Promising Responses to Changing Student Populations* (Rowman & Littlefield, 2017), *Literacy Leadership in Changing Schools: Ten Keys for Successful Professional Development* (Teachers College Press, 2016), and *Changing Suburbs, Changing Students: Helping School Leaders Face the Challenges* (Corwin, 2012).

She has published several articles and book chapters on topics related to the CSI mission, multilingual learners, leadership, and professional development schools. She and her PDS colleagues were awarded The Professional Development School Research SIG of the American Educational Research Association's (AERA) Claudia A. Balach Teacher Researchers Award (2018). She has a PhD from Fordham University in Language, Literacy, and Learning.

www.ingramcontent.com/pod-product-compliance
Lightning Source LLC
Chambersburg PA
CBHW061836300426
44115CB00013B/2399